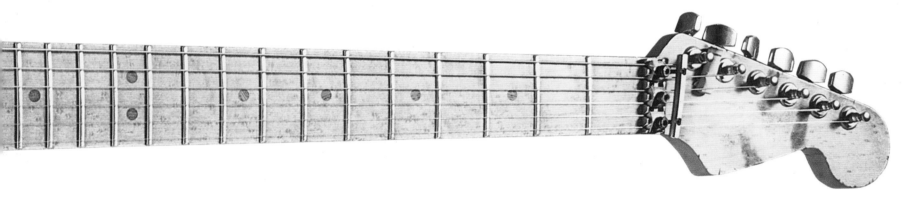

GUITAR
AFICIONADO

THE COLLECTIONS

The Most Famous, Rare, and Valuable Guitars in the World

Lindsey Buckingham at home with his
Rick Turner Renaissance 12-string

Time
HOME ENTERTAINMENT

Copyright © 2013 Time Home Entertainment
Inc.

Published by Time Home Entertainment Inc.
135 West 50th Street • New York, NY 10020

ISBN 10: 1-61893-095-8
ISBN 13: 978-1-61893-095-8
Library of Congress Control Number:
2013938718

Printed in China

We welcome your comments and suggestions
about Time Home Entertainment Books.
Please write to us at:
Time Home Entertainment Books, Attention:
Book Editors, P.O. Box 11016, Des Moines, IA
50336-1016

If you would like to order any of our
hardcover Collector's Edition books, please
call us at 1-800-327-6388, Monday through
Friday, 7 a.m. to 8 p.m., or Saturday, 7 a.m. to
6 p.m., Central Time.

Guitar Aficionado® is a registered trademark of
NewBay Media, LLC.

Cover/book design: Danielle Avraham

GUITAR
AFICIONADO

THE COLLECTIONS

The Most Famous, Rare, and Valuable Guitars in the World

EDITED BY TOM BEAUJOUR AND CHRISTOPHER SCAPELLITI

I hate to be the bearer of bad news, but the guitars

featured in *The Collections* are not magical. I should know. As the editor-in-chief of *Guitar Aficionado* magazine and the author of several chapters in this book, compiled from the pages of our publication, I have had occasion to play quite a few of them. Sadly, strumming the Gretsch White Falcon that belongs to the Black Crowes' Rich Robinson—shown at left—did not give me a sudden deep understanding of open tunings. Likewise, plinking away on Eric Johnson's 1957 Stratocaster failed to bestow my playing with a newfound fluidity. Most disappointingly, grabbing hold of Rick Nielsen's checkerboard Hamer Standard didn't instantly morph me into a power-pop songwriting ninja.

To me, the fact that these guitars, while indubitably precious artifacts, are not imbued with any inherent juju is a reassuring reminder of the individual artists' talents. And what those players have created with these instruments is nothing short of transcendent: songs, riffs, and licks that have been the soundtrack to our lives and a perpetual source of joy and wonder. And if you're a guitarist—as I suspect many of you are—the long hours you have doubtlessly spent trying to recreate those performances have probably produced some of the most immensely satisfying—and, alternately, frustrating—moments of your life.

With *The Collections*, we've endeavored where possible to have the players themselves explain what value, both tonal and sentimental, each instrument holds for them. You'll probably be surprised by how beat up some of the axes are, and how many modifications and repairs they have undergone. Some have been the victims of their owners' own frustrations and tinkering, while others have survived plane crashes, broken necks, thefts, and, in one case, being thrown into a fireplace by an unhappy spouse. The stories are unique, in some instances as much or more so than the guitars themselves.

I'd like to thank co-editor Christopher Scapelliti and designer Danielle Avraham for their efforts and unflagging composure in creating *The Collections*. Despite the fact that this was not a small project and was completed while everyone involved attended to his or her quotidian responsibilities, it was a blast to compile. As *Guitar Aficionado* continues to visit the homes and guitar dens of the world's greatest players to document their collections, the magazine will, as always, publish new, exclusive, and beautifully photographed features on the subject. If you enjoy what you see here, I strongly encourage you to visit the *Guitar Aficionado* web site, guitaraficionado.com, and subscribe to the magazine. There's much more to come!

Finally, with Christopher and Danielle's permission, I'd like to dedicate this book to my father, Michel Beaujour, who passed away in the months between when we first started gearing up for this project and its completion. I would have been proud to hand him a copy of *The Collections*. And if you knew how mercilessly professorial and critical he could be, you would understand that this is the highest praise I can give to this tome.

TOM BEAUJOUR
Editor-in-Chief
Guitar Aficionado

When I was a kid growing up in Rockford, Illinois, in the Sixties, there weren't books like the one that you're holding now, or magazines like *Guitar Aficionado* where you could find out everything about the cool guitars your idols played. I would scrounge for bits of information anywhere I could. In high school, I even had an airmail subscription to the British magazine *Melody Maker* so that music news from abroad would get to me while it was still fresh!

It was in that magazine that I first saw a tiny photo of Jeff Beck with a Les Paul guitar that had its pickup covers removed, revealing the double-white PAF pickups beneath. I had never seen those before. I figured that they were two Stratocaster pickups glued together, until one day, while looking through the edges of a pickup cover on a Gibson, I spied a glimpse of white lurking underneath. It was like, "Whoa!" (In a strange twist of fate, I actually ended up selling a sunburst Les Paul Standard to Jeff for $350 a few years later. You can read all about that on page 147.)

In the mid Sixties, when I began buying guitars that were made in the Fifties and early Sixties, few people thought that these instruments were better than what was available new. They were just "used guitars," not "vintage," and it was a great time to start a collection if you knew in what strange places to look for them. I would go to car dealerships, because people might have a Les Paul or some other model guitar and trade it in as a down payment on a new or used car. You could go out to the country and maybe a farmer would have a Gibson Firebird under the bed. He'd say, "Well, I don't know what it is, but I don't want it anymore, because it only has five strings left on it."

Since those earlier days and through the ensuing decades, I've continued buying, selling, trading, bartering, and collecting. More than 2,000 guitars and other instruments have passed through my hands, and I'm still learning to appreciate new things all the time. Today, I have more than 400 guitars in my collection, and I'm always on the lookout for other cool stuff. As you'll see in the chapter about my guitars, some are classic collectibles by Gibson and Fender, while others, like my checkerboard Hamer Standard and my original five-neck Hamer (it's the first of three that I now own), are products of my imagination that I had built for me. One thing that I'm proud of is that I've used most of these guitars and beaten the crap out of them on the road. Guitars are meant to be played, and they're happiest when they're making music, even if it means that they get a few dings, bruises, and breaks along the way.

Which brings me to the guitars in this book that *don't* belong to me. For the most part, these are guitars that my peers, my friends, and, in some instances, my heroes have used to write, record, and perform some of the greatest songs in the history of rock music. These aren't pristine museum pieces valued because they have never been played or are finished in some rare color that was used for just one day in 1967—these are guitars that have worked hard and have the scars and scratches to prove it.

So sit back, relax, and enjoy this book. I'll see you out on the road!

RICK NIELSEN
Guitarist, Cheap Trick

CONTENTS

THE COLLECTIONS

BEYOND THE COLLECTIONS
A Gallery of Legendary Guitars

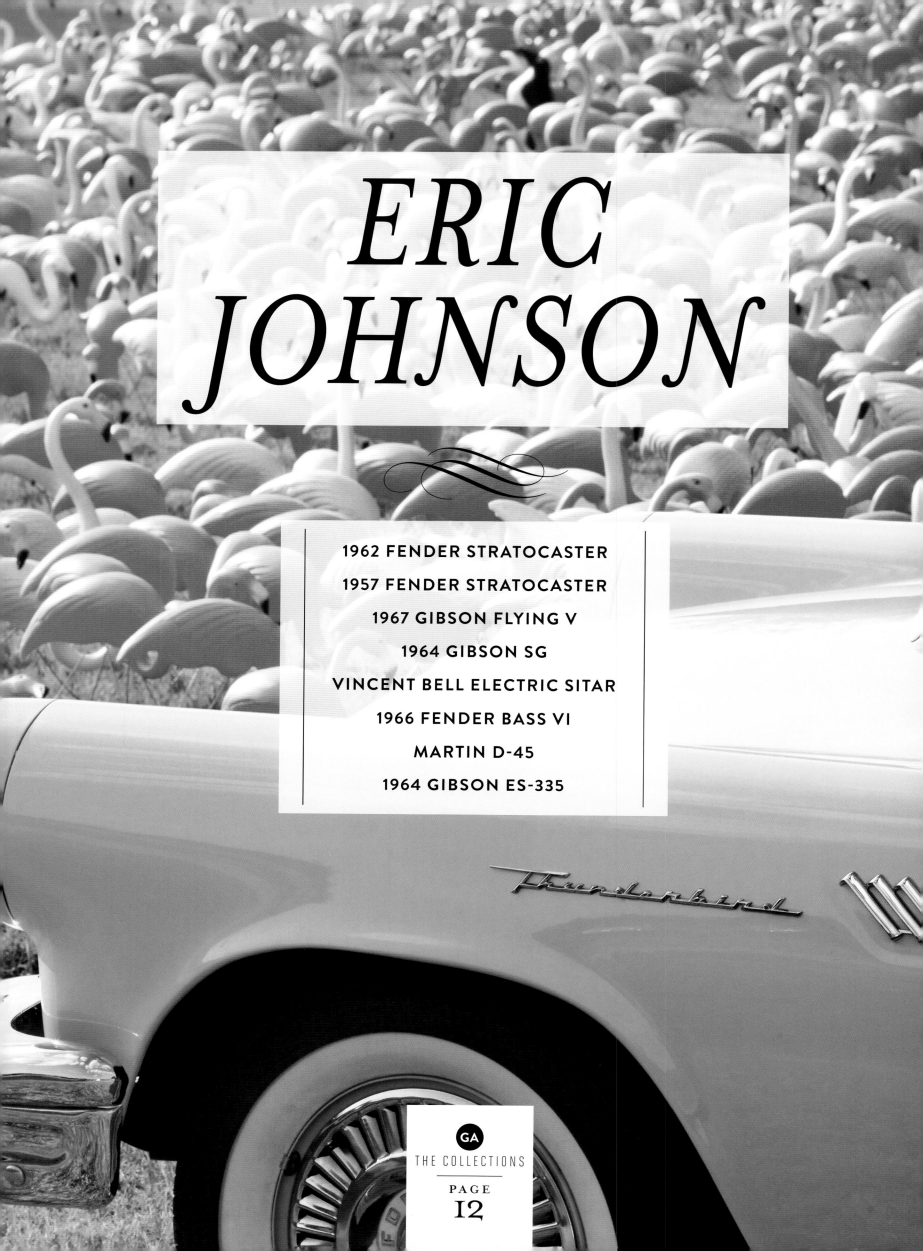

ERIC JOHNSON

1962 FENDER STRATOCASTER

1957 FENDER STRATOCASTER

1967 GIBSON FLYING V

1964 GIBSON SG

VINCENT BELL ELECTRIC SITAR

1966 FENDER BASS VI

MARTIN D-45

1964 GIBSON ES-335

Eric Johnson is sitting in the kitchen/lounge of his new

studio, Saucer Sound, considering the question just posed to him—specifically, why he chose to build his own recording studio. "Ever since I was a kid and discovered that Jimi Hendrix had a studio called Electric Ladyland, I've dreamed of having my own place," he says. The guitarist's dream has now become a fully operational facility, situated in the hills just west of downtown Austin.

It's here that Johnson recorded his soon-to-be-released new album, *Up Close*. Judging by the rough mixes for the lively blues "Vortexan" and a sweet ballad called "Arithmetic," the guitarist is comfortable enough in his new digs to take more musical chances and elicit more real emotion from his instrument than ever before. Johnson says, "I think that a lot of my songs had this potential that they didn't quite ever realize because they were being stifled by my being too cerebral about it. Now I'm trying to play the stuff live and give it more of an organic energy. I've listened back to a few of my records and realized that they're not really inviting to listen to. It's more like you observe them rather than feel them."

Johnson remains best known for "Cliffs of Dover," a track from his 1990 album, *Ah Via Musicom*, that earned him a Grammy for Best Rock Instrumental Performance and established his legend as a painstakingly meticulous and tone-conscious guitarist. But if Johnson's new studio has freed him from an overly analytical approach to his craft, his newfound desire to rely more on sense than science is also demonstrated in the way that he chose to design and fine-tune Saucer's large, linoleum-tiled live room. "We definitely tried

to create a specific vibe here," Johnson says.

To do so, he took a cue from Bill Putnam, "the father of modern recording," who in the Fifties created much of the equipment and established construction standards that defined studio technology and design for the post-WWII recording industry. Johnson says, "Putnam designed a lot of old rooms, like Ocean Way in Los Angeles, where the Beach Boys always used to record, and that facility had floors like this. And when he was fine-tuning a room, Putnam would just come in and use his ears and instincts, which is what we tried to do too. I mean, the acoustic treatment at Carnegie Hall was done that way 150 years ago. I think eventually they redid it the 'correct' way and they didn't like it as much."

Johnson certainly seems at ease when ensconced in Saucer. There he is surrounded by his favorite amplifiers (a stunning array of late-Sixties Marshalls and blackface Fender combos) as well as his collection of vintage guitars and several examples of both his

maple- and rosewood-necked Fender signature Stratocasters.

Of late, Johnson has thinned his collection, in part to cover the expense of building the new studio but also because he feels that, at this point in his life and career, he has neither the time nor inclination to be encumbered by superfluous possessions. "I've gotten rid of a lot," he says. "I just think that I'm not as interested in having a bunch of stuff I don't use anymore. Any guitar that I keep is like a transparent vehicle that'll just take me where I want to go and make music for me."

And these days, making music, not chasing an elusive perfect sound, is Johnson's top priority. In the two decades since *Musicom*'s release, he has completed studio recordings at a glacial pace and is now intent to make up for lost time. "I asked myself, What is it I wanna do; what is it that I wanna focus on?" he says. "Because you can't do it all. So me? I'd like to try to learn to make better music. For that, I only need a few nice guitars."

> **"I'd like to try to learn to make better music. For that, I only need a few nice guitars."**

In Saucer Sound with his 1957 Fender
Stratocaster; (previous page) with his
Eric Johnson signature Fender Stratocaster

1962
FENDER STRATOCASTER
(LEFT)

"I ONLY HAD THIS GUITAR for a year when it was stolen from my apartment back in 1982, along with several other great guitars. It was missing for 24 years. Then one day I was looking for a good old Ibanez Tube Screamer for a friend down at Austin Vintage Guitars and they showed me a few instruments that an old lady had brought in that had belonged to her husband. I started playing them and was suddenly like, 'Oh, my god, these are my guitars!' I had a record of all the serial numbers, so I ran home to check them, and these were all the guitars. The pickups in here are actually Fender Mustang pickups that I'd had rewound by Seymour Duncan to be a little hotter than Strat pickups. I think they read out at something like 6.5k."

1957
FENDER STRATOCASTER

"This is one of the two old Strats I have left. I was out on the road with my side project, Alien Love Child, about 10 years ago, and a guy brought this guitar to a soundcheck at a show in Florida. I was like, 'Sorry, man, I'm not interested,' and he was like, 'Just plug it in.' I did, and it totally blew away the 1960 rosewood-neck Strat I was touring with at the time. So I bought it and sold the '60 when I got home."

1967
GIBSON FLYING V

"I was at the Dallas Guitar show about 13 or 14 years ago, and even though I wasn't really looking for a V at the time, I stumbled on this one, and it just sounded great. The guy who had it would only trade it for a Thirties Dobro, so while I was trying to figure out how to get this guitar, my friend Eugene Robinson went and bought a Dobro at one of the other exhibitors' booths and sold it to me so I could get the V. I love that show. It's always got a great swap-meet vibe to it. The frets on this guitar are still original, and they're pretty gnarly."

1964
GIBSON SG

"I had a couple of really old pinstripe Marshall cabinets that I wasn't using and decided to unload. This guy offered to trade me his SG for them, and until then I really wasn't that into SGs, because every single one that I played wouldn't stay in tune for more than five minutes. But this guitar stays in tune, and it sounds great. You plug it in and it's instant *Wheels of Fire*."

VINCENT BELL ELECTRIC SITAR

"This is one that my father found for me. He had no idea how rare it is. I used it on *Up Close*. It's a very early model with no serial number and a 'Patent Pending' sticker. The only other person I know who has one of these is Steve Miller."

1966
FENDER BASS VI

"When my guitars were stolen in '82, one of the things that went was an early Sixties Bass VI. I was really bummed about losing that. About a week later, I walked into a pawnshop and saw this one, and was like, 'Well there's my replacement!' A lot of engineers hate me for using this thing, because it sounds more like a guitar than a bass, so they have to add a lot of equalization to make it work. But it does work! I used this on my last studio album, *Bloom*, on the track 'Tribute to Jerry Reed' and also on a country piece on *Up Close*."

MARTIN D-45

"Back in the late Seventies and early Eighties, Ray Hennig at Heart of Texas Music Store here in Austin had Martin make several pre-war D-45 copies for him, and my dad bought me this one after all of my other stuff was stolen. This is a very sentimental guitar to me. I was really pretty traumatized by that burglary at the time. I guess everyone is pretty naïve until something like that happens to them."

1964
GIBSON ES-335

"I bought this guitar from George Gruhn in Nashville 10 or 12 years ago when I was on tour with B.B. King, and it's my favorite Gibson that I own. I prefer the block-inlay, stop-tailpiece 335s to the earlier dot-necks. The pickups aren't quite as hot, but I prefer their sound. This guitar was spotless until Max Crace, the photographer who is shooting me and the guitars for this very story, dropped a loupe on it and dinged the top while he was creating the still life that's in the gatefold of the *Venus Isle* record."

DAVID CROSBY

1962 MARTIN D-18
12-STRING CONVERSION

2003 OLSON SJ

1970 GIBSON/ALEMBIC CUSTOM
ELECTRIC 12-STRING

1967 GIBSON ES-335

1930s GIBSON ROY SMECK
STAGE DELUXE 12-STRING CONVERSION

David Crosby owns more than 30 guitars, but he doesn't consider himself a collector. "I picked all my guitars because they helped me play," the two-time Rock and Roll Hall of Famer says. "They rang a bell inside me. Graham"—Nash, Crosby's longtime musical partner in Crosby, Stills and Nash—"picked a lot of his because of who owned them. He's got guitars that belonged to Johnny Cash and Duane Allman. Those are really worth something. But I don't have stuff like that. I've definitely spent a lot of time in pursuit of the perfect acoustic, but I didn't set out to collect, and I didn't purposely buy collectible guitars."

All the same, Crosby has acquired a rather valuable group of axes over the years, many of which adorn the walls of his rambling ranch house in the mountains of Santa Ynez, California. From a pristine 1927 Martin 00-45 to a dazzling 2003 Olson SJ, the collection has its emphasis on acoustic guitars, but there are a few cool electrics included as well, among them a 1967 Gibson ES-335 and an eye-popping custom 12-string built for Crosby by Alembic in 1970. Step into the adjoining garage and you'll find a pile of heavy-duty road cases containing what Crosby calls his "work guitars," meaning the models that he takes with him on tour, including three 1969 Martin D-45s. Two things you won't find, however, are the Gretsch Tennessean and Country Gentleman that he played live with the Byrds in the Sixties. "I've still got 'em," he says cryptically, "but they're not here."

The fact that he still has them—indeed, that he's hung onto so many of these instruments for such a long time—is something of

a surprise. Back in the dark Eighties, when Crosby was freebasing cocaine at a staggering rate, he sold a lot of possessions to feed his habit. And yet, for the most part, he kept the guitars. "One really good one went," he recalls. "A 1939 Martin herringbone D-28. I regret it tremendously. But it was a good life lesson. I learned that the answer is to hang onto them."

Crosby maintains that none of his guitars were bought to be mere home décor, but he acknowledges that some receive more attention than others. The two that get the most regular play are the ones he uses for songwriting, both of which hang from a custom rosewood wall stand near his bed. On the left is a 1962 Martin D-18, heavily customized to accommodate 12 strings. CSN's "Wooden Ships," among many other songs, was composed on this guitar, which was also the basis for Martin's David Crosby D-12 model— "the best production acoustic 12-string on the planet," says its namesake (he owns one of the four prototypes). Hanging to the

right of it is Crosby's current fave, a 1998 six-string concert model presented to him by its builder, Washington State luthier Roy McAlister. "I've always been a dreadnought player and stayed away from the smaller bodies," he says. "But this one nailed me to the wall. It's just scrumptious."

According to Crosby, his collection is complete at this point. "I'm not looking for any more guitars," he vows. "That said, anytime a really old Martin is in the offing, I'm still interested. But I don't want to pay half a million bucks for one, and ever since Stephen [Stills] paid [Nashville guitar authority George] Gruhn what he paid for his pre-war D-45,

the prices have gone right through the roof. I blame Stephen."

He laughs. "In the long run, I'll probably give a lot of my guitars away to other musicians. Having them is really nice, and I try, out of guilt, to play them all regularly, but some of them I just don't play enough, and they all should be played, truthfully. There are other guys out there who are better players than I am who do not have an ax of this quality, and they should. I've given a couple like that away. I'll meet somebody who's a superior player, but can't afford a really good guitar, and give them one of mine. The fact is that they were built to be played, not to hang on a wall somewhere."

> "I'm not looking for any more guitars. That said, anytime a really old Martin is in the offing, I'm still interested. But I don't want to pay half a million bucks for one."

Crosby with his Gibson/Alembic
custom electric 12-string;
(previous page) with his 1962
Martin D-18 12-string conversion

"I became obsessed with 12-strings,
but I didn't hear one that sounded better than
my D-18, so I decided to convert it."

1962
MARTIN D-18 12-STRING CONVERSION

"I WAS PLAYING FOLK CLUBS in Chicago in the early Sixties when I got this," Crosby says. "It was the first guitar I bought with my own money, and it must have been all of $300. At the time, of course, it only had six strings. Later, I became obsessed with 12-strings, but I didn't hear one that sounded better than my D-18, so I decided to have Lundberg's"—the legendary Berkeley guitar shop— "convert it. It took three tries before they got it right. They had to move the bridge; that's why the pickguard is there: to cover up the hole. And they put on a wider neck that joined the body at the 12th fret. That affected the bracing pattern and made an enormous difference in the tone. It's like a cannon."

2003
OLSON SJ

"Everybody that's ever played an Olson wants one," Crosby says. "They're astoundingly good, but they're expensive. Well, we got hired a while back by this lawyer to play a party that he throws every year. The guy was onstage afterwards, looking at my Martins, and he said, 'Do you have an Olson?' I said, 'No.' He said, 'You should have one.' I said, 'I don't think I can afford one.' He said, 'I'll buy it for you. Just go on their web site, pick one out, and tell me what you want.' Now I'm not a pushover—it took me at least half a second to say, 'Great idea!'" What Crosby picked out was a true beauty: a small-bodied single-cutaway with Brazilian rosewood back and sides, a cedar top, and a stunning dragon inlay on the fingerboard.

1970
GIBSON/ALEMBIC CUSTOM ELECTRIC 12-STRING

This one-of-a-kind ax has the laminated rosewood body of a 1970 Gibson Crest, a short-lived model similar to the ES-355. Mario Martello, a master luthier from the Bay Area, topped the body with a Brazilian rosewood neck and ebony fingerboard. The folks at Alembic did the rest: Ron Wickersham designed the onboard stereo preamp (making it one of the earliest guitars to use active electronics), while Rick Turner made the pickups and did the remainder of the body work, including the headstock logo, the brass and bronze additions, and the LEDs that run along the side of the neck, which still work perfectly 40 years later. "This is the first use of LEDs on a guitar in history," Crosby says proudly. "It's great for playing in the dark."

1967
GIBSON
ES-335

"I bought this one when I was still in the Byrds," Crosby recalls. "I walked into Wallach's Music City on the corner of Sunset and Vine one day, and there it was. I said, 'Gee, that's a really nice-looking guitar.' I loved it, and I still do, but I never got used to playing live with the whole Gibson two-volume-controls-in-series setup. Some people, like Neil [*Young*], can do magnificent things with it, but it's never worked for me. I kept it all the same, because it's a beautiful guitar, and of course nowadays vintage 335s are something special. Everything you see on it, including the Bigsby, was on there when I first got it."

1930s
GIBSON ROY SMECK STAGE DELUXE 12-STRING CONVERSION

Gibson produced the Roy Smeck Stage DeLuxe from 1934 to 1942, but the company never made one that looks quite like this. Originally a gift to Crosby from Jackson Browne, the guitar is the beneficiary of another Rick Turner 12-string conversion. As on the Martin D-18, the bridge has moved south and the neck has been replaced, but in this case the 12-fret neck is consistent with the design of the original Smecks, which were built as six-string Hawaiian guitars. Although the bridge has 12 holes, there are only six bridge pins, a feature that Crosby believes enhances tone. "Also," he notes, "I reverse the standard order of the low and high G-string pair on my 12-strings. It makes a difference when I do up-picking with my fingers."

RICH ROBINSON

1963 GIBSON ES-335

1967 FENDER TELECASTER

LES PAUL STANDARD

1975 GUILD F-512 SB

1963 GRETSCH WHITE FALCON

We wouldn't presume to know whether Rich Robinson is contented in all areas of his life, but where his guitar collection is concerned, this founding member of the Black Crowes is a sated man. "I pretty much have everything I could want," he says on a stormy late-summer night before the band takes the stage at Atlantic City's Borgata Hotel, Casino and Spa. "In fact, even though I know there are guys out there with three or four hundred instruments, I sometimes feel like it's silly to have even the 50 or so guitars I have."

Consider for a moment that Robinson tours with nearly 30 instruments (including backups) to accommodate the more than dozen altered tunings he employs on a nightly basis with the Crowes, and you'll realize that few of the guitars in his collection are sitting idle. And even those lesser-used instruments have at some point served Robinson well. "I think it was Neil Young who said every guitar has several songs in it, and I've always felt that way, too. Certain guitars—they could be vintage, they could be new—you'll pick them up and something about them will just click. With other guitars—you could pick up a '59 Les Paul, and it could be crap for you. The guitars that I've accumulated are those that I've always connected with."

Recently, the instruments that have been clicking with Robinson most are a pair of Gretsches: a 1963 White Falcon and a refinished 1957 Streamliner. The Falcon was one of the main guitars he used to record the band's new *Before the Frost... Until the Freeze*, a rootsy album recorded live before a select group of fans at the Woodstock recording studio of former Band drummer Levon Helm. "The Falcon has this bite on the high strings and warmth on the low strings that I really love, and that just feels good to me right now," says Robinson, who used a single tweed Fifties Fender Vibrolux for the recording. The resulting compressed, rounded tone is a stark departure from the overdrive that the guitarist employed on earlier Crowes records, and that mellowed growl fits perfectly on tracks like the Band-inspired "Good Morning Captain" and the stomping, swaggering "Kept My Soul."

Now that Robinson has all the guitars he wants and needs, he says that he would like to get his hands on two other stringed instruments: specifically, a harpsichord and a cello. "The cello is my favorite instrument," he explains. "That frequency really hits me. The sound of an old wood instrument that has been vibrating its entire life is unbelievable."

A painter for the past two decades, Robinson is stimulated equally by music and the visual arts. He counts a Salvador Dali first-run lithograph among his prized possessions and has purchased recent works by Spanish painter Sunol Alvar, British-born mixed-media specialist Catherine Farish, and New Orleans artist Ben Smith. Other favorites include Gerhard Richter and Gustav Klimt, whose *Portrait of Adele Bloch-Bauer I* sold in 2006 for a whopping $135 million. Robinson however, is adamant that he would never purchase a piece of art purely as an investment. "I don't buy things unless they move me," he concludes, "be they paintings or guitars."

> "I think it was Neil Young who said every guitar has several songs in it, and I've always felt that way, too. Certain guitars, you'll pick them up and something about them will just click."

Robinson with his 1963 Gretsch White Falcon;
(previous page) with his 1957 Gretsch Streamliner

"I don't buy things unless they move me,
be they paintings or guitars."

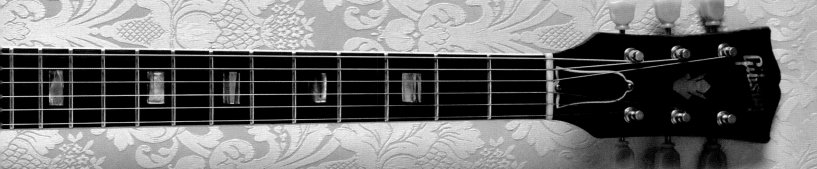

1963
GIBSON ES-335

"I HAD ALWAYS WANTED A good 335, and one day a guy brought this guitar to one of our shows. The second I plugged it in, I was like, 'Wow, this is amazing!' This instrument—the way that it sits and how it feels when I strum it—just feels like home to me."

1967
FENDER TELECASTER

"When the Crowes started out, we loved R.E.M., the Who, and the Jam, and the guitarists in all those bands played Rickenbackers, so naturally I played one too. I traded my Rickenbacker for this Telecaster right before we were going to record our debut, *Shake Your Money Maker*, with George Drakoulias and Brendan O'Brien. The guitar needed a fret job, and I wanted a humbucker in the neck position, like Keith Richards had, so I had a bunch of work done to it right away. I've used it on every record and tour since."

LES PAUL STANDARD

"I got this guitar for $400 at the same time as the Tele, because I'm also a huge Humble Pie fan and I wanted a guitar that was a little beefier. The finish was like this when I found the guitar, and someone had repaired the headstock and put some sort of heavy metal pickup in the bridge. By the time I got it, I didn't know what the hell this guitar was. Someone said it might have been a 1968 '56 reissue, but I really don't know. It's just cool."

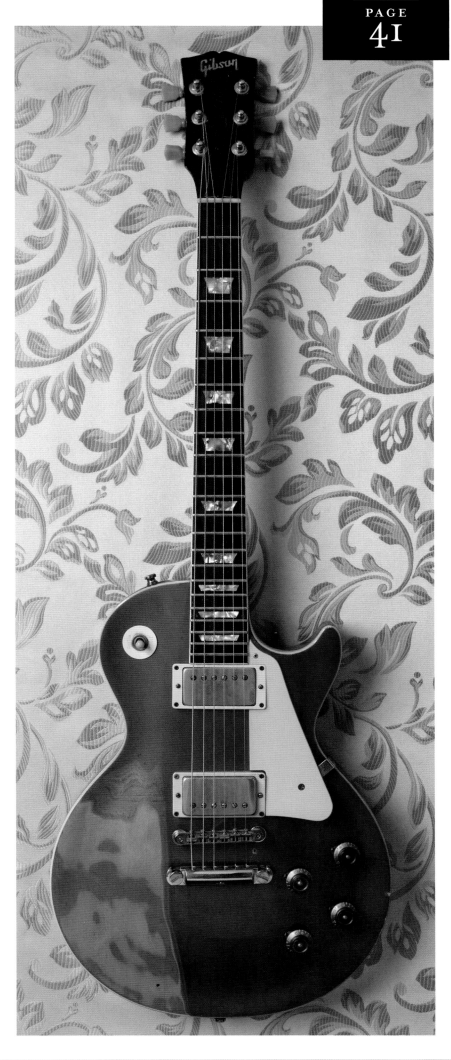

1975
GUILD
F-512 SB

"I had always wanted a 12-string, and I tried to find a Martin, but the ones that I played were just sort of dark sounding. Then, toward the end of the *Amorica* tour, I walked into Guitars R Us in Hollywood, and there was this Guild. It sounds great, and I've played it on pretty much everything that has a 12-string on it, starting with *Three Snakes and One Charm*."

1963
GRETSCH WHITE FALCON

"I'm a huge fan of Stephen Stills and of Malcolm Young, who used to play one of these, so I've owned White Falcons since *The Southern Harmony and Musical Companion* and sort of traded them up along the way. This '63 just sounds great, and it's in very good condition. I used it a lot on our new record, and I play it on at least four songs a night when we're on tour."

JIMMIE VAUGHAN

KAY BARNEY KESSEL
JAZZ SPECIAL

1962 FENDER STRATOCASTER

1958 FENDER STRATOCASTER

DANELECTRO LONGHORN
DOUBLE-NECK

KAY K161 THIN TWIN

1952 GIBSON ES-350

At a small guitar shop at the back of a strip mall on South Lamar Boulevard, in Austin, Texas, Jimmie Vaughan is admiring a patch of early Gibson acoustic archtops designed by the company's legendary chief luthier, Lloyd Loar. "This is the kind of stuff I like," he says, pulling his fingers across the strings of a particularly worn L-5. "I like guitars that are old and have a classic sound, something that you can't get out of the ones they make today."

Austin Vintage Guitars, is a wonderland of six-, eight-, and 12-strings of all years and models. But Vaughan has special business at the store on this day: retrieving a signature model Jimmie Vaughan Tex-Mex Stratocaster from the repair shop. After checking the fix-up job by playing a few licks through an old Fender Twin Reverb, Vaughan—sporting authentic Fifties sunglasses, head-to-toe black wardrobe, and trademark slicked-back hair—heads out to his muscular pickup truck. He gets in and drives, the guitar—*sans* case—riding on the back seat, like one of the hombres.

Vaughan's next destination is Top Hat Recording, the studio on the outskirts of town where he cut his new album, *Plays Blues, Ballads & Favorites*. Like the guitarist, Top Hat is decidedly retro. It has a well-earned reputation for its vintage gear, warm tube sounds, and recordings made on good ol'-fashioned two-inch tape. Its suburban ranch-house vibe was ideal for conjuring the album's laid-back grooves, which Vaughan spices up with jalapeño string work.

At 59, Vaughan admits that he picks and strums slower than he did in his years with the Fabulous Thunderbirds. "A friend

recently played me a CD reissue of *Butt Rockin'*, our third album, and I couldn't believe how fast we played," he says. But Vaughan has always had a reputation for putting the right note in exactly the right spot—and in a style that sounds like the second coming of Johnny "Guitar" Watson, Freddie King, Earl King, Jimmy Reed, and Albert King, all rolled up into one big, bad, blues hosanna.

That approach is smeared all over *Plays Blues, Ballads & Favorites*. And since this is Jimmie Vaughan, those favorites include classics like Reed's "Come Love," where Vaughan's Fifties-vintage Kay Thin Twin—strung, like all his guitars, with flatwounds—provides the era-perfect *chank*-ing rhythm. And then there's "The Pleasure's All Mine," a tune by Memphis proto-rocker Billy "The Kid" Emerson, on which Vaughan's bright Strat attack is as prickly as a porcupine in a cactus field.

But playing show-and-tell, not guitar, is on the agenda for this particular afternoon, as Vaughan has brought some of his favorite instruments to Top Hat to share with *Guitar Aficionado*. Most are his own rough gems—some battered and bearing the musical instrument equivalent of jailhouse

tattoos, others almost as shiny as the day they left the factory. He's also brought along a guitar that belonged to his kid brother, the legendary Stevie Ray.

"I'm not really a collector," Vaughan says. "I like old guitars and old cars. I play the guitars I own and enjoy driving my cars. I'd never buy anything for an investment."

For Vaughan, it's all about recapturing the magic of his Fifties and Sixties boyhood. "The world was quieter back then," he says, "yet it was such an exciting time. Music was changing, and cars and guitars were changing, and it was all part of the same thing—a kind of ultramodern and cool style, with gorgeous curves on everything, from rocket ships to the back fins of a '61 Cadillac."

It was during that time that he developed his affinity for the Stratocaster, the guitar with which he has been most associated throughout his long career. "I used to ride

the bus downtown to stare at them in the shop windows, because they looked like Corvettes," he recalls. "They were so beautiful in all their colors, lined up in a row. I used to dream about them." Some things never change: the Strat is still Vaughan's dream guitar. "With a good amp, if you know how to set your tone, it can do anything any guitar can do," he says, "from big jazz sounds to a steel guitar sound to all the shit in between."

Although Vaughan owns about 200 guitars, he's never acquired one solely because of its rarity or historic nature. "I use my guitars to recreate my own Top 40—the sounds I heard on records being played around Dallas in the Fifties and Sixties," he explains. "Those sounds were big and pure and honest. And if I can make other people feel the way I felt when I heard them, I think that moves beyond just making music and into something spiritual."

"I used to ride the bus downtown to stare at the Stratocasters in the shop windows, because they looked like Corvettes. I used to dream about them."

(here and previous page) With his 1958 Stratocaster. "I sat at the side of the road and carved my name into the wood with a beer-can opener. I thought, If somebody steals my guitar, they'll know whose it is."

"I'd never even seen a real Barney Kessel Jazz
Special. I'd just fantasized about owning one some
day. So this is one of my proudest acquisitions."

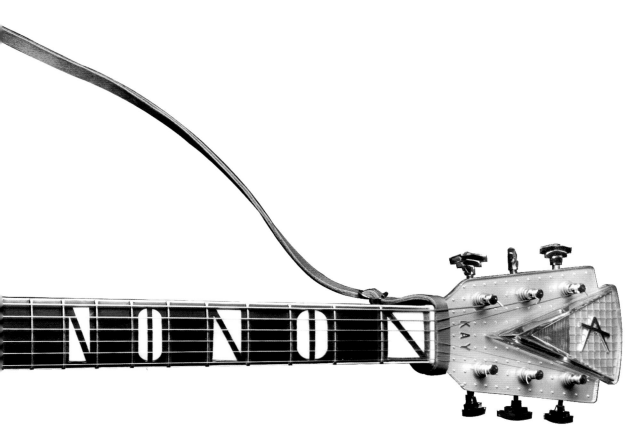

KAY BARNEY KESSEL JAZZ SPECIAL

"I LOOKED FOR THIS GUITAR for 10 years," Vaughan says, cradling the art deco–inspired beauty in his lap and gently picking a few soft, swinging phrases. "I've always loved the playing of Barney Kessel and the other classic jazz guys, and I wanted one of these since I saw a picture of one from a 1958 catalog. Kay made three Barney Kessels, including the Pro and the Artist models, but this is the top-of-the-line Kay, with the 'Kelvinator' headstock, Grover tuners, the chrome Melita bridge, silver acrylic pickguard and the 'Kleenex box' pickups. These pickups sound great. I like single-coil pickups better than anything else, and the old ones sound best. In its day, this was the poor-man's Gibson Super 400."

The guitar also has a rich, resonant unplugged tone that ripples from under Vaughan's fingertips as he moves them across the fretboard's split-block inlays. He's unsure of his Jazz Special's vintage, but the model was built in Kay's Chicago factory from 1957 to 1961. Purchased for $5,000 on eBay, it's one of his costliest acquisitions and a jewel in his collection. "Before I bought this guitar, I'd never even seen a real Barney Kessel Jazz Special," he says. "I'd just fantasized about owning one some day, so this is one of my proudest acquisitions."

"This is the second one," Vaughan says, pointing at the "Lady Luck" illustration on the guitar's back (at right). "You can see the outline of the one that wore away."

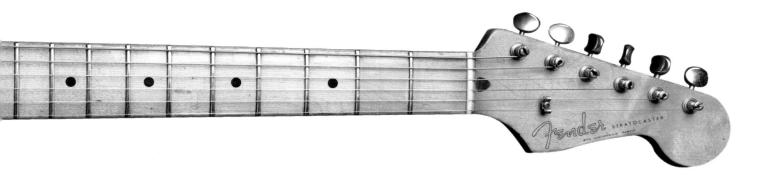

1962
FENDER STRATOCASTER

Vaughan's Olympic White 1962 Stratocaster may have more scars than Rocky Balboa, but he loves it anyway. "I used this guitar for most of the Fabulous Thunderbirds records," he explains, "and it's the one I modeled my Jimmie Vaughan signature model after, with all of the original modifications that Fender put in that guitar."

Those include medium jumbo frets, a gently V-shaped neck, hot-wound pickups in the neck and middle positions, and tone controls that bypass the middle pickup, which is reversed-wound to cancel hum. There is also, of course, a Vargas-girl-style decal on the back. "This is the second one," he says, pointing at his Lady Luck. "You can see the outline of the one that wore away."

Vaughan bought the instrument in his pre-Thunderbirds days, purchasing it from Texas string-slinger Bill Campbell for $200. Today it's kept in the same bank vault as his sunburst 1958. "It originally had a rosewood neck, and I put a maple neck on it as soon as I got it," he recounts. "By now it's had seven or so. This one's a Schecter."

Although this powerful workhorse is now permanently shedded, Vaughan has a strategy for reproducing its sound and feel on the road. "I like to buy Jimmie Vaughan signature model guitars when I find them used for a couple hundred bucks," he says. "The first thing I do is check to see if I need to replace the neck—because every individual guitar that comes out of the factory is always slightly different, regardless of what kind it is—and then we rewire the pickup selector so it works like a three-way. The original Jimmie Vaughan model came with a five-way pickup selector because that's what Fender had more of, but I like the three-way switch because that's the way they were on the vintage ones."

1958
FENDER STRATOCASTER

"This is my original '58 with a different neck on it," Vaughan says of the battered tobacco-sunburst ax that appeared on the cover of the Fabulous Thunderbird's second album, 1980's *What's the Word?* "It's the first Stratocaster that I bought, in the Sixties, for $175. The original neck wore out in the Seventies. It was shaved down and had a lot of wear and tear on it. I pay a lot of attention to the condition of my guitars' necks. They get worked on and shaved down over time and get too thin. I've had five or six different necks on it."

The guitar that Vaughan used on the Thunderbirds' dance-craze-inspired "The Crawl" and the swinging instrumental "Extra Jimmies" has three trapezoidal, metallic stick-on letters reading *JLV* above its pickguard. "I did that way before Stevie did," Vaughan says, referring to the familiar initialing on his brother's "Number One" Strat. "A lot of us hillbillies did that. In my old neighborhood in Dallas, everybody put those stickers on everything they had. Even cars."

But there's an even more distinctive "signature" on the guitar's back: "When I ran away from home and was hitchhiking to Austin, I sat at the side of the road and carved my name into the wood with a beer-can opener," Vaughan explains. "I thought, Well, if somebody hits me over the head and steals my guitar, they'll know whose it is."

DANELECTRO LONGHORN DOUBLE-NECK

When Jimmie and Stevie Ray's bands would share a bill, one of the highlights was the brothers' four-handed rendition of the surf classic "Pipeline" on a double-neck guitar. Often they used Jimmie's Strat-style ax, made by Robin Guitars of Houston, which he sold at auction for $45,410 to benefit Eric Clapton's Crossroads addiction treatment center. At other times, it was this Danelectro Longhorn double-neck, with a baritone neck on the bottom.

"I don't know much about this guitar, because it was Stevie's," Vaughan offers. "We were both photographed with it for the cover of *Guitar Player* when we recorded *Family Style*. This guitar and a bunch of other things—lyrics, Stevie's stage clothes, some of my amps and guitars—were stolen from my storage space in 2007. They took a long list of stuff. Somebody fixed the door so it looked like it was locked when I saw it, but it was open, and they were able to help themselves. I had a couple of wardrobes that were Stevie's, and they would go in and take song lyrics and clothes and sell them and come back for more. They would arrange things so it looked like nothing was missing. This went on for a while, until I heard that some of Stevie's things I knew I had were being sold. I hired a detective and got most of them back."

KAY K161 THIN TWIN

This guitar was immortalized on 2007's *On the Jimmy Reed Highway*, where Vaughan joined his gravel-throated Texas compatriot Omar Kent Dykes in paying tribute to the late blues hitmaker. But the tone-chambered K161 model's chunky sound was cast in stone decades ago on classic recordings like Reed's "Big Boss Man" and John Lee Hooker's "Boogie Chillen'." Both men, along with Howlin' Wolf, were famously photographed with these blonde blues machines.

The guitar is another example of Kay's genius for discount chic. The ripple of the three-ply flamed maple top shines through its light finish and is complemented by a zebra-striped tortoiseshell pickguard that extends over the tone and volume knobs. Reissues come with a chrome bridge and adjustable saddles, but Vaughan's is the real deal, with an old-school wooden bridge—less functional, but ideal for the vintage tones he craves. The same goes for the so-called "iceberg" pickups—the thin metal blades on the surface hide the thick stacks of windings and magnets below that give the K161 its kick.

Kay built the Thin Twin from 1952 to 1959. Vaughan isn't sure when his example left the factory, but, he says, "when you plug it in and start playing, the years roll back."

1952
GIBSON ES-350

As much as Vaughan loves Strats—and that would be a lot—the first guitar he ever fantasized about buying was an ES-335. "I already owned some pawnshop Telecasters, which were perfectly fine guitars," he says. "But ever since I heard Freddie King play 'Hide Away,' I wanted to get an ES-335. I planned to get one in 1966, when I went out shopping for the first guitar I bought new with my own money."

Instead, thanks to a salesman who wowed the budding bluesman with B.B. King licks, Vaughan walked out with an ES-330 that he paid for on an install-ment plan cosigned by his father, Big Jim. He still has that guitar today, plus other models from the ES family, including this ES-350.

"Chuck Berry played the ES-350 before he switched to the thinner models. I wanted one of these since the first time I saw him, and I finally got this guitar about 11 years ago," Vaughan says, resting the vintage Gibson on his lap and plucking a few slow phrases that reveal a rich, hefty tone. "I still have the bill of sale in the case, from Fretware Guitars in Franklin, Ohio. I saw it listed in an ad in a guitar magazine and called them up and ordered it sight unseen."

LINDSEY BUCKINGHAM

1974 GIBSON LES PAUL

1980 RICK TURNER MODEL ONE

2004 TURNER RENAISSANCE

1969 MARTIN D-18

1960s FENDER STRATOCASTER

Distinguished looking and graying at age 61, Lindsey
Buckingham has achieved an ideal balance in his professional and personal life. "I've got this big machine, which is Fleetwood Mac," he says, "and this small machine, which is my solo work. The solo work is how you really keep growing as an artist. But then I can feed that growth back into Fleetwood Mac."

The guitarist has been focused on his small machine of late, having just released his sixth solo album, *Seeds We Sow*. It's an understated yet compelling distillation of his distinctive songcraft, singing, and guitar work—artfully wrought layers of vocal harmony and sparkly guitar tones that showcase his unique fingerpicking style. His production aesthetic can be quirky, placing tricky crossrhythms or supercompressed drums in surprising places. But most tunes inevitably get down to one of those sunny, mile-wide choruses that remind you of Buckingham's role as chief tunesmith behind the hitmaking juggernaut that is Fleetwood Mac.

For all that, though, *Seeds We Sow* has an intimate and personal feel that reflects Buckingham's current life situation: happily married with three kids, his wild years of rock and roll excess behind him. Nestled in an upscale L.A. suburb, the house he shares with his wife, Kristen, son William Gregory, and daughters LeeLee and Stella is idyllic and homey, a two-story edifice of white brick and white shaker shingles, with a gabled roof and verdant ivy climbing the walls. A spacious lawn and meticulously kept gardens are laid out in casual, easygoing symmetry. But Buckingham himself doesn't seem to be much of a gardener. Pausing to contemplate a clump of well-groomed green-

ery alongside a walkway, he muses, "What's that? Rosemary?"

Inside, a tasteful medley of ornately inlaid Indian furniture, European rococo, and chinoiserie pieces create a comfortably inviting atmosphere. Everywhere you look, there are coffee-table art and photography books on the works of Picasso, Max Ernst, Cartier-Bresson, Annie Leibovitz, and others. Also ubiquitous are floral prints—on upholstery, wallpaper, and other surfaces—suggesting, perhaps, a woman's touch.

Trim and blonde, Kristen Buckingham is an avid horsewoman. She was once thrown and badly injured but bravely got back in the saddle soon thereafter. She prefers this mode of exercise to yoga or gym. "I get bored unless it's some kind of game," she says.

"I was really lucky to meet this beautiful lady," Buckingham says, beaming. "The odds of having children didn't seem that likely at my age. We had our first child when I

was 48, which is a pretty late start. And it's been a great gift, especially to have gotten into it after all the other garbage I've been through."

He's alluding, of course, to Fleetwood Mac's coked-up heyday and the tumultuous, public breakup of his relationship with singer Stevie Nicks, which provided much of the subject matter for the band's multi-Platinum album *Rumours*. "All through the late Seventies and Eighties, the rock culture was in fairly constant party mode," Buckingham says. "I think everyone thought that they were doing what they had to do. It wasn't unusual. But as a result, I saw a lot of my friends who were parents who weren't there for their children most of the time. Or when they were there, they weren't setting a good example. I didn't want to be one of those people. A lot of those kids grew to have, shall we say, issues."

Which is the underlying theme of *Seeds We Sow*. "Who you are as a person is a sum total of the choices you

> **"Who you are as a person is a sum total of the choices you make, and sometimes it's hard to know if you've made good or bad choices until time has given you a perspective on it."**

With his Rick Turner
Renaissance 12-string;
(previous page) with his
modified Rick Turner
Model One

make," Buckingham says, "and sometimes it's hard to know if you've made good or bad choices until time has given you a perspective on it."

The new album was recorded entirely in Buckingham's home studio, located in a separate building just steps away from the main house. It too is quaint, white, and ivy-clad on the outside, but it's far more spartan than the main house on the inside: a working space equipped with a Pro Tools rig, a Neotek console, a Sony 48-track digital tape machine, and a cache of guitars. Buckingham did most of the playing himself on *Seeds We Sow*, sheepishly admitting that a good deal of the drum sounds came from GarageBand. For him, solo work is the yin to Fleetwood Mac's yang. He compares making a Fleetwood Mac album to making a movie. It's a large-scale production, with plenty of moving parts and creative egos to be brought diplomatically into accord.

"What makes Fleetwood Mac a great band is that we really have no business being in a band together," he says with a laugh. "The synergy of all the disconnected parts makes the sum bigger than the whole. But Fleetwood Mac is also a brand that you have to uphold. Say you're Ridley Scott and you're making the next *Pirates of the Caribbean* film: it's a brand, and there's nothing very chancy that can be done within that, because there are expectations that go along with it."

By comparison, solo work is for Buckingham more like the act of painting. "It's meditative," he says. "It's solitary; it's not communal. This is where you can take risks and follow your heart. You have a canvas to fill. You may not have a song; you're just kind of slopping colors around, and gradually something comes into focus. As opposed to being conscious, it's subconscious. The lyrics emerge from somewhere underneath. You may not know what you're saying until you're done. And sometimes not even then."

Just as our life choices shape who we are as people, our guitar choices shape our sound and style. Buckingham isn't a guitar collector,

per se. He doesn't acquire them for their beauty, rarity, or market value; they are his tools. But the instruments in his collection trace the story of his life and career: playing steakhouses and coffee shops as one half of the up-and-coming duo Buckingham/ Nicks, as a member of multi-Platinum hit-makers Fleetwood Mac, and as a mature solo artist and sonic auteur.

"What makes Fleetwood Mac a great band is that we really have no business being in a band together. The synergy of all the disconnected parts makes the sum bigger than the whole."

With his 12-string Rick
Turner (left) and 2004
Rick Turner Renaissance

"It was a great guitar for leads and some other things,
but it wasn't really suited to my playing style."

1974
GIBSON LES PAUL

PURCHASED AT THE HOLLYWOOD LOCATION of Guitar Center, this is the guitar Buckingham played during the period of *Rumours, Tusk,* and other classic Fleetwood Mac discs. The tuners and pickups have been replaced, and a sizable chunk of the white finish has come off the side of the headstock—all signs of heavy use. Nonetheless, Buckingham is not particularly fond of the instrument and confesses that some of the wear on the guitar may have come from his flinging it down on the stage in frustration.

"Before Stevie [*Nicks*] and I joined Fleetwood Mac, I was using mainly Stratocasters and Telecasters onstage," he explains. "But when we joined Fleetwood Mac, they had a pretty interesting sound, which was much fatter. And suddenly those very clean, percussive Fender guitars did not fit in. So I had to find something else, which was this white Les Paul.

"It was a great guitar for leads and some other things, but it wasn't really suited to my playing style. It took me a few years, but I realized I wasn't getting the most out of my style. The band was trying to get me to start using a pick. I said, 'That's not what I do!' So I knew I had to find another guitar."

1980
RICK TURNER MODEL ONE

The solution to Buckingham's Fleetwood Mac guitar dilemma came from luthier Rick Turner. The two men met in 1979 during sessions for Fleetwood Mac's album *Tusk*. Turner, then transitioning out of Alembic and setting out on his own, had been building gear for Mac bassist John McVie and would stop by the studio.

Buckingham recalls, "I said to Rick, 'Make me a guitar that in your mind would be right in the middle between a Gibson and a Fender—something that has some of the fatness of a Les Paul but also has that real clean kind of percussive thing that a Fender would have.' So that's what he came up with."

This particular Turner guitar shows signs of heavy wear and modification over the years, indicative of Buckingham's obsessiveness over tone. There are at least two dowels set into the body where potentiometers once were, and there's heavy cracking around one of the existing knobs. "I must have used it as a baseball bat at some point," Buckingham muses.

2004
TURNER RENAISSANCE

Seated in his living room, Buckingham plays a mellifluous fingerpicked passage from his song "Shut Us Down" on this guitar, which he has tuned to open G. "That song was a lot more tame on record than it ended up being onstage," he says. "But I wouldn't dream of playing anything other than this guitar for that. Playing a D-18 or a Taylor, it's not the same thing. This Turner Renaissance has an orchestral evenness and gives back more of a rock and roll thing than any dreadnought-size or other traditional acoustic. It's basically geared to be an electric guitar with a closed acoustic body. You plug it in and it just rocks. And there's a lot of that kind of stuff on my new album. There's one song called 'Stars Are Crazy' and another called 'Seeds We Sow.' Those were both done on this guitar."

While the Renaissance was not created specifically for Buckingham, he can clearly see his influence on Turner's design aesthetic. "I think Rick and I have some kind of psychic link," he says with a laugh. "And it flows both ways."

1969
MARTIN D-18

Buckingham purchased this guitar when he was 18 or 19 years old and has used it for performances and recordings throughout his career. It is an instrument on which he began developing his signature finger-picking style while still quite young. "I bought it at a place called Guitars Unlimited in Menlo Park, in the San Francisco Bay area," he recalls. "That's where Jerry Garcia used to hang out before the Grateful Dead were the Grateful Dead. I used to see him in there all the time. I picked up this guitar and just held onto it all this time."

1960s
FENDER STRATOCASTER

This Fender Stratocaster is another guitar that has been with Buckingham throughout his career. "I played bass in the one band I was in after high school," he says, "because I wasn't a lead player at the time and I didn't have the gear. But the guitarist in that band loved to take guitars apart and work on them, and he had this one sitting around. He actually just gave it to me." Buckingham stripped off the finish when he was in his twenties. Much later on, Rick Turner installed an Alembic gain boost.

RANDY BACHMAN

1950s ROGER SUPER CUTAWAY

1968 FENDER LTD

1970s GRETSCH SUPER AXE

1970 "HARDTAIL" FENDER STRATOCASTER

1950s LES PAUL CUSTOM

HOYER BIANKA

As guitar collectors, we regularly sing the praises of

instruments made in the late Fifties. But when it comes to single-engine aircraft of the same vintage that are about to transport us over a wintry Pacific Ocean, we are not equally enthusiastic.

Nervously eyeing the 1958 DeHavilland Beaver floatplane that will take us from Vancouver International Airport to Salt Spring Island—the home of guitarist Randy Bachman—we are having second thoughts about paying a visit to one of classic rock's guitar greats. Our pilot is busy balancing on a bobbing pontoon while loading an overweight bag into the cargo hold, but he senses our trepidation. "Don't worry," he says with a confident grin. "These things run forever if you maintain them properly. They're so simple that nothing can really go wrong!"

Once aloft, we realize our reservations were for nothing. The DeHavilland is a breathtaking way to make the trip to Salt Spring Island, a destination that lies in the Strait of Georgia, between mainland British Columbia and Vancouver Island. In addition to being the largest and most populous of the surrounding Gulf Islands, Salt Spring is a popular vacation destination in warmer months, with a thriving gourmet locavore movement, multiple vineyards, and artisans galore.

And then there's Bachman's homestead. A short drive from the village of Ganges, where our pilot has safely deplaned us and our photographic gear, the lakeside compound of the former Bachman-Turner Overdrive and Guess Who guitarist features several wooden structures, including a main house with fortress-like

curved walls, a small guest house, and a barn that has been converted into a recording studio, where he recorded his most recent album, *Bachman & Turner*, with former Bachman-Turner Overdrive cohort Fred Turner. The sprawling home, commissioned by Bachman and his wife, Denise, in 1998, is a stunning showpiece of eco-friendly design and construction techniques. The walls and bulk of the structure are fashioned of rammed earth, an ages-old construction material that has recently regained popularity among homebuilders concerned with sustainability issues. The house's wooden beams are made from recycled railroad trestles and the remains of an old logging bridge, and the space is geothermally heated and cooled via a closed loop of pipes that circulate water underneath the adjacent lake and floors.

As he guides us through his airy living room, where an in-ground goldfish pond gurgles and a fire roars underneath a large mantle, the man whose writing credits include such ubiquitous rock hits as "Takin' Care of Business," "You Ain't Seen Nothin' Yet," and the classic "American Woman" seems restless, as if conversation about the sumptuous

decor is an unwelcome distraction. But once he escorts us into his office, all seems right in Bachman's world, and with good reason. An entire wall of the room is covered with the fruits of his latest collecting obsession: German archtop guitars from the Fifties. Among the treasures are handcrafted specimens from such storied builders as Hoyer, Lang, Todt, and Rossmeisl.

"After the war, a lot of guys who had previously made symphonic instruments were starving, and they started to make guitars, because Django Reinhardt was big," Bachman explains. With materials difficult to obtain in postwar Germany, the builders were forced to improvise. As a result, the number of German archtops manufactured was small, and most have unique features. "The Hoyer and Hopf factories weren't even factories, more like garages," Bachman explains. "It was a father-and-son business. These guys just sat around and carved all this stuff, and it was just amazing. They would make maybe one or two or three a year. The tops would vary, too, because the builders couldn't always get the same woods when it came time to make another guitar."

While Bachman's collection of

"The greatest guitar you can get is the one that isn't available."

Warming up at home
with a stunning Hoyer;
(previous page) on his Salt
Spring Island homestead
with a Hoyer Special SL

German archtops continues to grow every day, it pales in comparison to the unrivaled collection of Gretsches that he recently parted with. "I sold my entire collection, which I had been accumulating for about 25 years, to Fred Gretsch," Bachman says. "I had hundreds of them—every Gretsch you could imagine. I even had prototypes that Gretsch didn't know existed. I had the only White Falcon bass, ever. As you can imagine, when those were gone there was kind of a void, and to fill that void I began buying German guitars."

The Gretsch collection itself was assembled to fill the void created when Bachman's favorite guitar, a Gretsch 6120, was stolen about 25 years ago. "I got that guitar as a teenager," Bachman says. "To get the $400 for it, I babysat, I had a paper route, I mowed lawns, I washed cars. I played it on my first hit record, 'Shakin' All Over,' with the Guess Who, in 1965, and on 'Takin' Care of Business,' almost a decade later, with Bachman-Turner Overdrive.

"Everywhere I went with it, I carried a double length of chain and two padlocks. When I had to leave my hotel room, I took that guitar into the bathroom, and I'd put the chain through the handle and around the body of the case and around the toilet and around the sink, and then around the guitar again, and I'd put the two padlocks on it. If someone wanted to steal it, he'd have to rip the plumbing out of the floor.

"Then one night, after a BTO session, my roadie says, 'I'm going to take your guitar now, then check out of the hotel, and we'll drive you home tonight.' He goes back to the room, packs his bag, leaves his bag at the door, leaves my guitar at the door, goes to the desk to pay, comes back five minutes later, and the Gretsch is gone. I threw up. I couldn't sleep. It was like your dog being run over, or a losing-your-girlfriend kind of thing. Incredible."

Bachman mounted a campaign to recover the guitar, and on the advice of the Ontario Provincial Police began contacting pawnshops. "I contacted every pawnshop, first in Toronto and then in Ontario. When that didn't

This fine example features both *f*-holes and a center soundhole; (right) a wall of Bachman's German archtops

pan out, I went through the Yellow Pages for every town and city in the U.S.A.; I would find every pawnshop and write to them, asking if they had the guitar." Bachman never recovered the guitar, but his correspondence with a vast network of pawnbrokers yielded offers to purchase many other instruments. "They'd call me and say, 'We didn't find your orange Gretsch, but we did get another weird white one that you could have for $200.' So I'd buy a guitar, buy a guitar, buy a guitar. Suddenly, I had six on the wall, and I had the bug."

The finely honed guitar-hunting skills that Bachman developed by searching for his Gretsch have served him well in his quest for rare German archtops. With the aid of his daughter, he prowls the U.S. and German eBay sites in search of good buys, and even uses electronic bidding software to ensure that he wins as many auctions as possible. "There are still great finds out there, because American collectors aren't really hip to these guitars yet," Bachman says.

And if the prices on German archtops become as prohibitive as those of vintage Gretsches? It's safe to say that Bachman will probably find another type of instrument to focus his attention on. "The greatest guitar you can get is the one that isn't available," he says half jokingly.

"They'd call me and say, 'We didn't find your orange Gretsch, but we did get another weird white one that you could have for $200.' So I'd buy a guitar, buy a guitar, buy a guitar."

"Roger Rossmeisl went to Fender in the late Sixties
and designed the LTD, which, as you can see, also
features that distinctive German carve on the top."

1950s
ROGER SUPER CUTAWAY (TOP)
1968 FENDER LTD (LEFT)

"ROGER GUITARS WERE MADE BY the German luthier Wenzel Rossmeisl," Bachman explains. "His son's name was Roger. This was Wenzel's top-of-the-line instrument, and it's absolutely a work of art. The lamination of the woods on the neck is just stunning, as is the carving of the top. Roger moved to the United States in the mid Fifties and worked at Rickenbacker. He then went to Fender in the late Sixties and designed the LTD, which, as you can see, also features that distinctive German carve on the top. They made 12 of these before Fender decided that they were too expensive and stopped production. Mine, which I got from J. Geils, is the 12th. Roger then designed the less-expensive Fender Montego, which also failed, as well as the Coronado."

1970s
GRETSCH SUPER AXE

"This is one of the only Gretsches that Fred Gretsch didn't get when he bought my collection," Bachman says. "Chet Atkins had read in *Rolling Stone* magazine about my 6120 being stolen and decided to call me. The first two times he called, I was out in the backyard, building a tree house for my kids. My daughter came out and said what sounded like, 'Chad is on the phone and wants to talk to you,' I thought she was talking about Chad Allen from the Guess Who and told her to say I'd call back. The third time the phone rang, she came back and said, 'He really, really, really wants to talk to you. He's calling from Tennessee and he's got a weird accent.' So I went to the phone, and he said, 'Howdy, this is Chet.' I could barely speak, because this was my idol. He asked me, 'Did you ever get back the 6120?' I said, 'No, I'm never gonna get it back.' And he said, 'Okay, what's your address?' Four days later, this Super Axe shows up. The string tree was a mod that Chet did himself, because the strings kept popping out of the nut."

1970
"HARDTAIL" FENDER STRATOCASTER

"I got it from Bob Heil, who developed the Heil Talk Box," Bachman says. "This is the guitar I played on 'You Ain't Seen Nothin' Yet' and 'Lookin Out for #1.' People ask me if I played a Les Paul on those tracks, but it's this Strat on the neck position. It used to have a Canadian flag sticker on it, and if you look at the back of the neck, you'll see that I took off the finish and sanded the neck like a violin, because violin was the first instrument I played. I've done this to several of my Strats, because I do a lot of sliding and find the stock finishes to be a bit too tacky sometimes."

1950s
LES PAUL CUSTOM

"Around 1974, I walked into a store in Westchester, Pennsylvania, and saw this and another Custom with P-90s hanging on the wall and asked if I could play them. Phenomenal! I asked if they were for sale, and the guy said, 'Not really. Keith Richards' roadie brought them in for fret jobs about two years ago and no one ever came to pick them up.' I told the guy that since the work was not paid for, he could invoke a mechanic's lien, where you send the owner a letter saying that you're entitled to be paid for your work, and that if you're not, you can sell the instruments. I asked the guy to send a registered letter to the Stones' label, which he did, and then a few months later he sent another one, neither of which they responded to. So the guy was free to sell the instruments. I once had to take a pickup out to fix something, and out came a matchbook from the Bag O' Nails in London, which is a club where the Stones used to play."

HOYER BIANKA

"The first time I saw a Hoyer Bianka, I thought, Those sound holes look exactly like the lightning bolt painted on David Bowie's face on the cover of *Aladdin Sane*!" Bachman recalls. "The back of this guitar is scalloped, just like the top, which like most of these guitars features a 'German carve' that goes in on the edges. This compresses the sound inside, and it makes for a really unique tone that cuts through on any track I'm recording. It's like it's got its own built-in EQ—tight but crisp, with a lot of upper midrange."

ELLIOT EASTON

1961 GIBSON BARNEY KESSEL CUSTOM

2004 GRETSCH ELLIOT EASTON
"WHITE TIKI" PROTOTYPE

1966 FENDER ELECTRIC XII

1967 FENDER MALIBU ACOUSTIC

1960s FENDER VILLAGER 12-STRING

1965 GIBSON ES-335 TDC-LH

2006 ELLIOT EASTON SIGNATURE MODEL
SG CUSTOM PROTOTYPE #1

2007 GIBSON HISTORIC LES PAUL REISSUE

2006 MARTIN ELLIOT EASTON SIGNATURE MODEL

When asked to pinpoint when they fell in love with the instrument, most rock guitarists reveal that the infatuation began in their early teens. But the affinity exhibited itself much earlier for Cars guitarist and avid ax collector Elliot Easton. "My mother always loved to tell the story about when I first saw Elvis on television in 1956 when I was three years old," Easton recalls, relaxing in the backyard of his suburban Los Angeles home. "After the show was over, I brought her a comb and a glass of water and I had her comb my hair in a spit curl. I stood in front of the mirror with a Mickey Mouse guitar and never looked back!"

The young Long Island native was not only precocious—he was also left-handed. Easton quickly realized that while some lefties could simply adapt to right-handed guitars, he preferred to play instruments that were either purpose-built or modified to accommodate his southpaw. "First I had an inexpensive Japanese guitar that we bought in a department store," he says. "I figured out barre chords upside down, and then I realized that there would be a lot of things I couldn't do. So I took the guitar into a local mom-and-pop music shop and had them turn the nut and strings around for me. That's when I really started learning how to play."

Easton's first bona fide left-handed guitar was an acoustic made by Favilla, a firm that manufactured ukuleles and other stringed instruments in New York City from the 1890s until the company moved to Farmingdale, Long Island, in 1962. (Entertainer Tiny Tim was one of their most notable ukulele endorsers.) "My local music store in Long Island was

this place called Gracin's Music, and they had a left-handed all-mahogany Favilla guitar in the store," Easton recalls. "I rode my bike every day to a job at a bagel factory to earn the money for it."

After logging many hours on the Favilla, it became clear to the young guitarist that if he hoped to accurately reproduce the sounds that he heard on his favorite recordings, he would need an electrified instrument—specifically, a Fender Telecaster. "I was crazy about the Band. My hero was Robbie Robertson, and he played a Telecaster," Easton says. "I also loved Jesse Ed Davis with Taj Mahal, and Bakersfield country players like James Burton and Roy Nichols, and they all played Telecasters. So in 1971, I got a job washing dishes in a restaurant and saved up $225 for a custom-ordered lefty Fender Telecaster. I drove Gracin's nuts, because I would call the store every single day to see if the guitar came in."

Despite his appreciation for the Telecaster, Easton's eyes (and ears) soon wandered to Les Pauls.

"I was a Mike Bloomfield freak, and that Les Paul tone on the *Super Session* album was just the greatest thing I ever heard," he says. "My high school band won a countywide battle of the bands, and our prize was a $500 gift certificate to Sam Ash. There were five guys in the group, so we each got $100 to spend. For whatever reason, there were several left-handed Gibsons in the store at the time, and I settled on a Les Paul Deluxe. I sold my Telecaster for $150, so that was $250 with the winnings, and my mom made up the rest. That Les Paul cost $297 with the case out the door, and I regretted buying it almost immediately because you couldn't do all the pedal-steel bends and stuff you could do on a Telecaster. I wanted a Fender again, but because I could only afford to have

one guitar at a time, I just went back and forth like that for years."

By the time the newly signed Cars traveled to England to record their 1978 self-titled debut album with producer Roy Thomas Baker, they were generating enough cash from their Boston-area gigs for Easton to have assembled a three-guitar arsenal: a Martin D-35 acoustic, a 1977 Les Paul Standard that he had refinished in red, and a new Fender Telecaster fitted with a Bartolini Hi-A mini humbucker in the neck position. Armed with those, a Morley Echo Volume pedal, and a Roland Chorus Ensemble, the guitarist cut all of his tracks, including the impeccably composed and executed solos to "Just What I Needed" and "My Best Friend's Girl," in less than two days. "That record took 12 days to make in total,"

"You have to find a very particular kind of customer to buy a high-ticket left-handed guitar. First, you have to find a lefty."

(here and previous page) At home with an Elliot Easton Signature Gibson SG Custom

Easton says. "It was our club set, and we knew what we were going to do, so we just went in there and regurgitated our parts onto tape."

The Cars turned out to be a hit, and Easton's new high profile dictated that leading manufacturers like Dean and Hamer were more than happy to accommodate his requests for special-order left-handed instruments. "Companies usually offer only their two or three most popular guitars in left-handed models, and that's it," Easton says. "But now I had a little bit of clout, because I was in a band that was selling records, and I could give a guitar company like Hamer or Dean some exposure if they built me a custom lefty."

In addition to acquiring new, custom-built instruments, Easton began to accumulate vintage left-handed examples, many of which were brought to Cars shows by local dealers. "That's how it was in the Seventies and Eighties," he says. "Vintage dealers would show up in the dressing room with guitars. They knew I was a lefty, so if they had a lefty in their inventory, they'd bring that to show me. I bought a 1964 Burgundy Mist Stratocaster that was unplayed, with the tags, the strap, and the payment installments receipt. It was in a white Tolex case that creaked when you opened it because the leather wasn't broken in yet. That guitar was $2,200, which was a fortune at that time. I paid under two grand for a '59 slab-board and $600 for a Lake Placid Blue '65 Tele."

By the time the Cars reconvened with Baker to record their second effort, 1979's *Candy-O*, at Cherokee Studios in Los Angeles, Easton had accumulated several dozen guitars, all of which were employed on the album. "I had all of them out on stands, and they just looked so cool," he recalls. "Before I ever reached for a guitar or an amp or a pedal, I would visualize the sound for a given part in my head and I would inevitably go to the right guitar, the right effects, and the right amp."

With that, Easton rises and leads us past the swimming pool and into his home, a Hacienda-style house that was built in the mid Seventies. The sun-drenched living room features a vaulted, A-frame ceiling and is decorated in immaculate midcentury mod style. "I'm a Sixties kid," Easton says, explaining his preferred décor. "I always have been and always will be. Some of the Scandinavian modern designs from the Fifties and Sixties, with their clean lines and beautiful wood, are just perfect.

"If they could have frozen the world in 1966 or something, in terms of pop culture and cars, that would have been fine with me," he continues. "And it's not that I'm trying to live in the past; it's just that I love some of those artifacts and the feeling that they generate. There was a sense of whimsy in the world, or at least in this country. We had plenty of money, and people were having fun. There were terrible things going on, of course, but it seemed like there was more of a capacity for silliness. Just think of things like Pillsbury Funny Face drinks like Goofy Grape, Jolly Olly Orange, and Choo Choo Cherry. We had such fun stuff."

Most of Easton's fun stuff—at least to guitar collectors—resides in a home studio that features wall-to-ceiling storage closets faced with richly figured Macassar ebony doors. More than 100 instruments are housed here. Some are rare vintage examples, while others are custom lefties built especially for him. (Factoid: After the Fender Custom Shop opened in 1987, two of the first 10 guitars it built were ordered by Easton: a Foam Green Telecaster Thinline and a "Mary Kaye" Strat with a bird's-eye maple neck.)

While the collection remains vast, the guitarist has thinned his herd a bit over the years, and many of the instruments that he accumulated during the Cars' Eighties heyday are now gone. Parting with instruments is not something that Easton relishes, not only because of the bonds that he forms with his guitars but also because unloading a lefty, no matter how rare, is never an easy task. "You have to find a very particular kind of customer to buy a high-ticket left-handed guitar," Easton explains. "First, you have to find a lefty—there aren't that many of us. And then it has to be a lefty who has the money to buy something like that."

Easton is also quick to point out that because there is comparatively little demand for left-handed vintage guitars, their extreme paucity is also not reflected in their price. "You'd think that because there are so few lefty vintage guitars, they would be worth exponentially more," Easton says. "It's like, I have a mint '58 Telecaster, lefty. How many of those could there be. Maybe three? If a righty is worth $30,000 and there's thousands of them, this lefty has to be worth $100,000 because there's none of them, right? But it doesn't work that way, because lefties are harder to sell and have a much smaller market."

And while he has parted with a few of his favorite and most significant pieces in the years between the Cars' dissolution, in 1987, and their reformation in 2010, Easton seems to have no regrets. He certainly loves the instruments, both new and old, that he has retained and continues to collect. As he opens one storage cabinet after another in an attempt to pick out a few guitars for our shoot, *GA* tells him to focus primarily on the instruments that he likes most.

"That's the problem," he says with a wide grin that's almost certainly identical to the one he sported when first seeing his Telecaster at Gracin's decades ago. "There isn't a single guitar here that I don't like!"

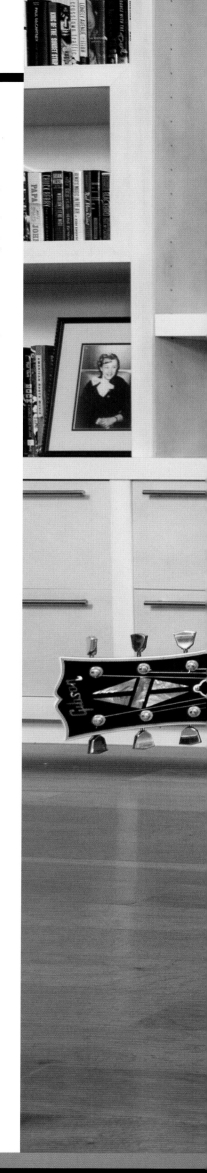

> "You'd think that because there
> are so few lefty vintage guitars, they
> would be worth exponentially more.
> But it doesn't work that way."

In his living room with a
left-handed Gibson ES-355

"It's the finest-sounding electric jazz guitar I've ever
owned, and it just nails that 'Wes tone.'"

1961
GIBSON BARNEY KESSEL CUSTOM

"THIS IS FROM THE FIRST year of issue, with PAFs, a laminated spruce top, factory Grovers, and a brown Lifton case with pink interior! Although some players and collectors don't care for the big double-cutaway shape, I love it. It's the finest-sounding electric jazz guitar I've ever owned, and it just nails that 'Wes tone.'"

2004
GRETSCH ELLIOT EASTON "WHITE TIKI" PROTOTYPE

"This is literally a one-off prototype; no other exists in the world. I had this idea to bring out a fancier, more deluxe version of my Gretsch signature model Duo Jet. Obviously, guitar fans will see it as similar to the White Penguin model, but the 25-inch scale, B7 Bigsby and Tune-o-matic bridge on studs rather than the typical wooden base make it a much more usable instrument. Of course, the best features are the gold plaque on the headstock that says 'Elliot Easton Tiki Model' and the tiki on the pickguard, courtesy of the great graphic artists at House Industries."

1966
FENDER
ELECTRIC XII

"I've had this one since the Eighties. It's a '66 and incredibly rare in a left-handed version. I've taken it to many sessions and it always records like a dream. Both Page and Townshend loved this model."

"That's how it was in the Seventies and Eighties. Vintage dealers would show up in the dressing room with guitars. They knew I was a lefty, so if they had a lefty in their inventory, they'd bring that to show me."

1967
FENDER MALIBU ACOUSTIC

"I love these Roger Rossmeisl–designed Fender acoustics, even though they're not very popular with players. While not as rich sounding as a Martin or Gibson, these have their special charm and record really well. This is also a great guitar for Nashville high-strung tuning."

1960s
FENDER VILLAGER 12-STRING

"This one is from the same era as the Malibu. It has the infamous metal support tube to keep it from caving in under pressure. Again, it's not the big, full sound of a Guild, Martin, or Gibson, but it's still very characterful and excellent for recording."

1965
GIBSON
ES-335
TDC-LH

"A minty '65 ES with factory Bigsby! In lefty! I've had it for around 15 years, and it is one of the good ones. Unlike later skinny-neck '65s, this one has the full-width neck, making it a superb player. It's one of the finest guitars I own."

2006
ELLIOT EASTON SIGNATURE MODEL SG CUSTOM PROTOTYPE #1

"I had this idea for a two-pickup SG Custom. I believe that the SG Custom is one of the sexier solid-bodies ever produced by Gibson but feel that most players favor the standard model because that third middle pickup crowds the real estate around the picking area. When Gibson changed the Les Paul shape to this double-cutaway design in 1961, they kept the Custom as a three-pickup model, even though the single-cutaway Black Beauty was often seen in the two-pickup configuration. I never understood why Gibson didn't make the same change when they went to this SG shape, so I took it upon myself to finally get Gibson to offer the two-pickup option on an SG Custom. The Vibrola tailpiece has the same tiki design seen on the pickguard of the Gretsch. Also, notice the 'split-block' inlay at the headstock—it slants the other way for the lefty model, something I don't think Gibson has done before or since."

2007
GIBSON HISTORIC LES PAUL REISSUE

"This one started life as a tobacco 'burst, but I always wanted a 'Sweet Cherry' and also love the look of George Harrison's red Les Paul. I sent the guitar off to RS Guitarworks for a new finish, Jensen oil-and-paper caps, RS SuperPots, and True 60s PAFs exclusively made for RS by Lindy Fralin. It's a great Les Paul, and changing those components made a huge difference in the tone. It's much more open sounding and very sensitive to the touch. Very dynamic."

2006
MARTIN ELLIOT EASTON SIGNATURE MODEL

"I always felt that Martin gave short shrift to the 'hog models by dressing them down with more austere, plain-Jane appointments: dark binding, less purfling, fewer fingerboard inlays, et cetera. I just wanted to give mahogany its props and dress it up a bit. Basically, it's an HD-28V with a few changes: Adirondack top, quilted mahogany back and sides, herringbone rosette, gold Waverlys, all gloss—including the neck—old-style decal, and all the usual prewar forward-shifted scalloped braces. The recipe works. It's the mahogany lovers' dream Martin dreadnought!"

NEIL GIRALDO

1960s GUILD STARFIRE III

1980s B.C. RICH EAGLE "KATO"

1978 B.C. RICH EAGLE

1940s MARTIN 000-18

1960s FRAMUS ACOUSTIC

1959 FENDER STRATOCASTER "VEGAS"

When Neil Giraldo was growing up in Cleveland, he didn't appear to have

many career options. "My father was a Sicilian carpenter, and that's what he wanted me to be," says the 57-year-old guitarist. "But I couldn't figure out a two-by-four from a two-by-six. So my choices were limited. All I knew is I could make music better than I could do carpentry."

After years of making music with local acts, Giraldo landed his first professional gig as a member of Rick Derringer's band. On his one album with Derringer, 1979's *Guitars and Women*, Giraldo mostly played keyboards, but his time with Derringer led to an important development in his guitar life. "When I first started playing with Rick, all I had was an SG," he recalls. "But he said to me, 'You need to play something different. I use a Mockingbird, so let's contact B.C. Rich and find something that you like.' And that's how I started using the Eagle, which is the guitar I became known for."

Not long after, Giraldo landed the position he still holds today. "I did the album with Rick and I got a call from someone I knew at a record company, saying, 'We just signed this girl to a deal. She wants to form a partnership with a guitar player.'" That girl was Pat Benatar. "I met with her in New York," Giraldo says, "and the rest is history."

Over the course of his more than 30 years with Benatar, he and the singer have racked up an impressive number of hits—"Heartbreaker," "Hit Me with Your Best Shot," "Promises in the Dark," and "Love Is a Battle-field," among many others—as well as multiple Platinum records and Grammy awards. They married in 1982. "It was meant to be," Giraldo says of their personal relationship. "There was no way that was not going to happen. We were together 24 hours a day and we got along so well."

In addition to his work with Benatar, Giraldo put his stamp on several other indelible Eighties hits, the most famous of these being Rick Springfield's "Jessie's Girl," on which he played all the bass and guitars as well as the famous solo (although the part is mimed by Springfield in the video for the song).

Since then, Giraldo has lent his talents to a variety of artists, including John Waite, Kenny Loggins, and the Del-Lords. Currently, he says, "I have a lot of different little bands and side projects that I'm involved in. I'm doing a Christmas record of all original songs with my good friend [*Dictators, and former Del-Lords, guitarist*] Scott Kempner. And then Patricia [*Pat*] and I will be doing new product as well." As for the many artistic hats he wears, Giraldo says, "We have a studio here at home, and whenever I go in there, I always think of myself in terms of being a writer and an arranger and a producer before an actual player. I think of the song first. Then I just pick up tools as I need them, whether it's a guitar or a keyboard or drumsticks. Whatever's in reach."

In his moments at home when he's not making music, Giraldo has of late also revisited the craft of his father. "If I'm not in the studio, I've got my construction tool belt on and I'm making things around the property," he says. "After all these years, I've actually become a builder. When I was younger, I couldn't figure out how to use a hammer. Now I'm building stuff all day long. I'm a ranch guy. I like to work hard; I like to work physical. Right now I'm working on a tool shed and a garage."

He laughs. "But what always happens is, I'll be building something and I'll get an idea for a song. So I'll drop the tool belt and run to the studio, pick up a guitar and lock myself in there for a couple hours. Then I'll put down the guitar, come back out and start swinging a hammer again." In between hammer swings, Giraldo was gracious enough to invite *Guitar Aficionado* into his and Pat's Malibu home to view a selection of the instruments that have shaped his sound over the years.

> "I always think of myself in terms of being a writer and an arranger and a producer before an actual player."

(here and previous page) On his ranch
with his early Sixties Guild Starfire III

"I bought this a long time ago and never
used it. It was like a keepsake. Then I
decided, It's time to break this out."

1960s
GUILD STARFIRE III

"WHEN I WAS A KID, there was a guitar player named Phil Meglarino who lived down the street in Cleveland," Giraldo recalls. "He had a great quiver. When he shook a string, it had a great sound. And he played a Starfire. When it got to the point that I had some success and I had some money, I wanted to get one of those guitars in honor of Phil. So I bought one a long time ago and never used it. It was like a keepsake. Then I decided, It's time to break this out. So as of the last couple years I've been playing this one. It came with a Bigsby, but I have a problem with the sliding bridges because I palm the bridge so much that it moves around. So I changed out the bridge and the tremolo."

"The gig was so horrible that I took the guitar and threw it in the trash bin in my storage space. Well, it stayed in that trash bin for, like, 15 years."

1980s
B.C. RICH EAGLE "KATO"

"The story behind this guitar is kind of cool," Giraldo says of the Eagle he named in honor of the *Green Hornet* character. "I used it for a gig at the Universal Amphitheatre [*now the Gibson Amphitheatre*] in L.A., back when it was an open-air place. I was maybe drinking a little too much, smoking too many cigarettes, and the gig was so horrible that I took the guitar and threw it in the trash bin in my storage space. Well, it stayed in that trash bin for, like, 15 years. Finally, the space was being cleaned out, and some guys said, 'Hey, Spyder [*Giraldo's nickname*], did you own some green B.C. Rich guitar?' So it came back to me. It was in bad shape. And I felt so bad seeing it that I reconstructed it. I also added Seymour Duncans, and Seymour always winds up something a little special for me. And now I have a whole new love affair with it."

1978
B.C. RICH EAGLE

This sunburst Eagle is one of two models Giraldo received from B.C. Rich when he began playing with Rick Derringer (the other, a maple example, was later stolen in a New Jersey club). It was his number-one guitar for many years. "I used this guitar on so much stuff," he says. "The whole *Crimes of Passion* record, 'Jessie's Girl'—it was my go-to guitar, my baby. It's also the one you see in a lot of those videos. Later on, I think in the early Nineties, I added the Bigsby. I bastardize guitars. They all have blemishes to them. It's part of who I am. As soon as it gets in my hands, it gets beat up. I'm not a protector of the original state."

1940s
MARTIN
000-18

"I've used this on just about anything that has an acoustic guitar on it," Giraldo says. "I bought it at Norman's Rare Guitars. He had a tiny little shop at that point, a boutique-y kind of place. He wasn't really well known then; there were no Internets. You'd go in there and see these guitars, and you'd fall in love with them. I love the lower-number Martins because they're really tight sounding. They have a great midrange. And I'm an aggressive player, so I wanna bang it out, and I want the midrange and all the strings to be equal in volume. And this guitar gives me that. It's like another piece of the drum kit."

1960s
FRAMUS ACOUSTIC

This beater guitar, which Giraldo says he bought for $99 in 1980, is also one of his most prized instruments. "I've written all kinds of songs on it—'Promises in the Dark,' 'Hell Is for Children'—so many things. It's my go-to songwriting guitar. I put the humbucker in myself, because I wanted to hear what it would sound like distorted through an amp," he says. "Another thing that makes it interesting is it's been stolen twice and returned twice. I lent it to a good friend of mine. He had it in the backseat of his car. Somebody broke into his car and took it. Then he got it back. Then I lent it to somebody else, and that person had it in their trunk, went into a restaurant, came out, and it was gone. I ended up getting it back *again*. The guitar just won't leave me. And it has a great soul to it. Every time I pick it up, I get inspired."

1959
FENDER STRATOCASTER "VEGAS"

"This guitar basically looks like a vintage tabletop," Giraldo says. "I went to a friend's house in New York, and he had this old Fifties table with a black finish and gold sparkles. And I thought, Wow, that would look really cool on a guitar. So I took this Strat, which was so beat up, and I did it myself. I put all kinds of junk on it. Mixed some black paint and gold glitter and made it look like the table. I used it for the *True Love* record [*in 1991*] and tour. It was on [*1993's*] *Gravity's Rainbow*, too. I've used it quite a bit. There's a Seymour Duncan Hot Rails in the back pickup slot. I wanted to get a more distorted, less Strat-y kind of sound. I also have another Strat in red sparkle that I call Reno."

ROBBIE ROBERTSON

1958 "BRONZE" FENDER STRATOCASTER

2010 "INDIAN" FENDER STRATOCASTER

2008 ROBBIE ROBERTSON SIGNATURE
"MOONBURST" FENDER STRATOCASTER

1928 MARTIN 000-45

1961 GIBSON DOUBLE MANDOLIN

1960s EPIPHONE HOWARD ROBERTS

"Guitars have their own character, their own identity,"

reflects Robbie Robertson, sitting at the legendary Village Recorders studio in Los Angeles, in a room filled with his instruments. "They all do different things; they sound different and feel different. You use them in the same way that golfers use golf clubs...or something." He laughs. "Actually, I've never used that analogy before."

If you wanted to run with the golf club analogy, you could say that Robertson—a guitarist, songwriter, and film composer, and the former co-leader of the Band—is more of an iron man than a wood man. From the Band's landmark 1968 debut, *Music from Big Pink*, to the new *How to Become Clairvoyant*—his first solo disc in 13 years—Robertson's musical game plan has consistently been about well-considered short strokes rather than fairway-clearing drives. When *Music from Big Pink* emerged at the baroque height of the psychedelic era, the subtlety of his work both as a guitarist and a songwriter was nothing less than revelatory, and it caused countless contemporaries—including Eric Clapton and the Beatles—to immediately reconsider their approach to music.

"When you're young, you tend to overplay a little bit," Robertson says. "So when I was in the Hawks"—the precursor to the Band—"and we did our first tours with Bob Dylan, I was still in this wailing mode. I was a kid on a mission. But by the time the Band made *Music from Big Pink*, I was leaning in the completely opposite direction; it was all about the subtleties. I was just in such admiration of how Miles Davis would play one note and it would be more effective than somebody else playing 20. And I admired Curtis Mayfield, and Steve Cropper on those Otis Redding songs.

"That kind of guitar playing became very appealing to me," he continues. "It was all about leaning on the songs, with very little in regard to jamming or playing solos just to put a solo in. And that was like going in the opposite direction [*of music*] at the time. But that's when people like Eric Clapton heard us and said, '*That's* the business! *That's* what to do!' At the time, it did have an effect on people, and I've kept searching in that mode for things ever since, not trying to be different but avoiding the obvious and embracing the unexpected."

On *How to Become Clairvoyant*, Robertson is joined by numerous guests, including Steve Winwood, Tom Morello of Rage Against the Machine, Trent Reznor of Nine Inch Nails, and funk/soul pedal-steel whiz Robert Randolph. But it's Eric Clapton who makes the biggest contribution, perhaps repaying his musical debt from 43 years ago. Clapton penned the album track "Madame X" and co-wrote two others, "Fear of Falling" and "Won't Be Back." Moreover, his enthusiasm for the project—and certainly his guitar playing and choice of instruments—significantly shaped the album.

"This project started with Eric Clapton and me," Robertson explains, "and Eric has an extraordinary ability: whoever he's playing with, he can adjust to that attitude quickly. On this album, I wanted to avoid acrobatics. When we were recording these tracks, we had it set up so that he and I were just sitting in front of one another, playing together. And when I was playing in this more subtle place, *he* was playing in a very subtle place.

"All the solos that we did with those tracks were done live. When we would finish singing and doing our subtle things between the lines, and it came to a solo, it was like the guitars were picking up right where the vocals left off. It was like 'talking guitars.' He'd say something and I'd say something, or he'd have a little monologue and I'd answer it with a little monologue. There was a particular thing going on, a mature, more grown-up way of us dealing with playing back and forth. It was never like, 'Oh, I'll show *you* something.'"

Robertson graciously agreed to show *us* something, however—his wonderful and historic guitar collection. From a 1928 Martin to his iconic bronzed Stratocaster to a brand-new Strat with an eye-popping paint job by Apache artist Darren Vigil Gray, his instruments have one thing in common: like the man's music, they're all evidence of Robertson's signature style as a guitarist and aficionado of fine stringed instruments.

> "I was in such admiration of how Miles Davis would play one note and it would be more effective than somebody else playing 20."

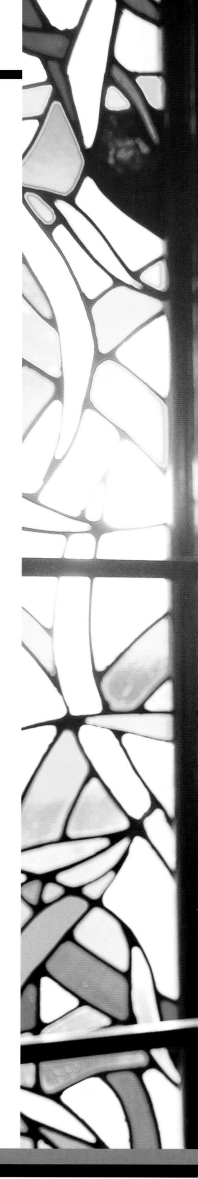

(here and previous page) With a
Gibson Style O guitar

"When we were preparing to do *The Last Waltz*,
I thought, I should do something for the occasion,
and I had it bronzed."

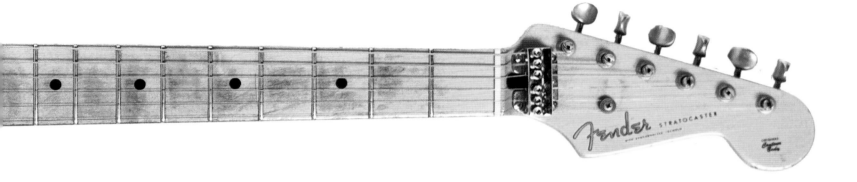

1958
"BRONZE" FENDER STRATOCASTER

THE MOST ICONIC OF ALL of Robertson's guitars, this bronzed Strat was his main ax for *The Last Waltz,* Martin Scorsese's documentary of the Band's lavish 1976 farewell concert. "The guitar was originally red," he says. "I used it on the tour with Bob Dylan in 1974. I used it on [*Dylan's*] *Planet Waves,* which we recorded with him right before we went on tour, and it's on *Before the Flood,* the live album from that tour. But when we were preparing to do *The Last Waltz,* I thought, I should do something for the occasion, and I had it bronzed. They dipped the body in bronze, just like they do with baby shoes. They dip it in, leave it for a minute, and then take it out. So then they put the guitar back together again, and it had a completely different sound to it. [*laughs*] Just like you would think, it had a more metallic sound. And I liked the sound I got out of it, but it was heavier. I'm pretty sure I also used the bronzed one on a couple of things on [*the Band's 1977 album*] *Islands,* but after that it was put away."

"It's just a classic Stratocaster, but it has the old Telecaster knobs, and it has lipstick pickups, and the hardware is all brushed gold."

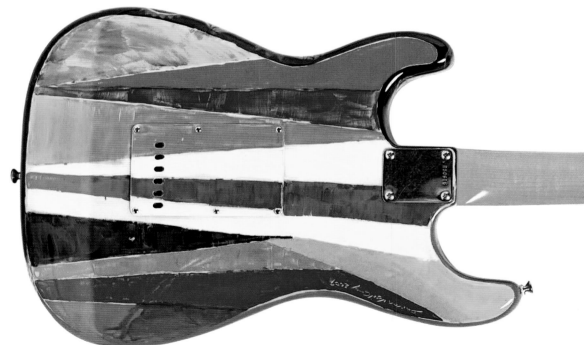

(Back of guitar)

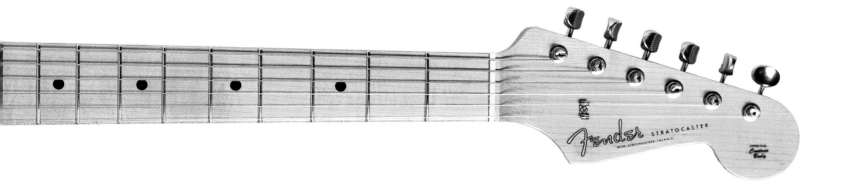

2010
"INDIAN" FENDER STRATOCASTER

"Darren Vigil Gray, a friend of mine from Santa Fe, New Mexico, painted this one," Robertson says of this addition to his Stratocaster arsenal. "The people at Fender asked me if there was a Native American artist who could do a guitar, and I told them that Darren would be the guy, because he's a great artist, he's Apache, *and* he's a musician. It's a piece of art," Robertson says of the final result. "It's just a classic Stratocaster, but it has the old Telecaster knobs—the ones that are round on top, not the flat ones— and it has lipstick pickups, and the hardware is all brushed gold. And against this Indian artwork, it's just a beautiful thing."

2008
ROBBIE ROBERTSON SIGNATURE "MOONBURST" FENDER STRATOCASTER

"This is the guitar that I used the most on this album," Robertson says of his 2008 signature Stratocaster. "It's called Moonburst because there's so much white and harvest-moon color in the finish." The hardware is unique, as well: Robertson replaced the standard Strat volume and tone knobs with Telecaster knobs, which he finds easier to manipulate while playing. "I do a lot of volume knob stuff with my little finger," he says. "One's a volume knob, and the other's an overdrive volume, and then there's one tone knob for everything."

1928
MARTIN
000-45

"That guitar is all over this record," Robertson says of this gut-string beauty, which he and Eric Clapton both played on *How to Become Clairvoyant*. "It's a magnificent instrument. Eric was the one who really kind of pulled me into its magic. He'd been playing it on some other things, and he was like, 'Oh, my god, the tone of this!' Its back and sides are made of Brazilian rosewood. It's like having a piano with keys made out of real ivory."

1961
GIBSON DOUBLE MANDOLIN

Robertson can be seen playing this gorgeous—and extremely unique—double-neck on "The Weight" in *The Last Waltz*. Unlike most of the "double-mando" guitars that Gibson produced in the late Fifties and early Sixties, which paired a short-scale six-string neck in the upper position with a standard neck in the lower, this one has an eight-string mandolin neck in the upper position. "In the mid Seventies, I got a bunch of guitars from Norman Harris of Norman's Rare Guitars, and this was one of them," Robertson says. "It sounded beautiful, it looked beautiful, and I liked the idea of having a mandolin handy like that. So I bought it from him, and then a few years later he came back to me and said, 'Listen—I found out something about that guitar, how really rare it actually is, and could I get that back from you?' I said, 'You know, that's probably not going to happen.'"

1960s
EPIPHONE HOWARD ROBERTS

If this archtop hollowbody looks familiar to you, it might be because Robertson is pictured strumming it on the inner gatefold of the Band's eponymous 1969 effort. Robertson says he stumbled across the instrument at a guitar store in Hollywood while on a break from sessions for the album, which took place in Los Angeles. "I went into the store, and it was just the best-looking guitar in there," he recalls. "I said, 'Wow, look at this beauty— this'll get me laid!' [*laughs*] We had rented Sammy Davis Jr.'s house in the Hollywood Hills, and we made the record in his pool house. So in that picture on the record, I'm just showing off my new guitar. I was like, 'I better use it on something!'" Robertson wound up playing the guitar on "When You Awake," one of three tracks that he co-wrote for the album with Richard Manuel.

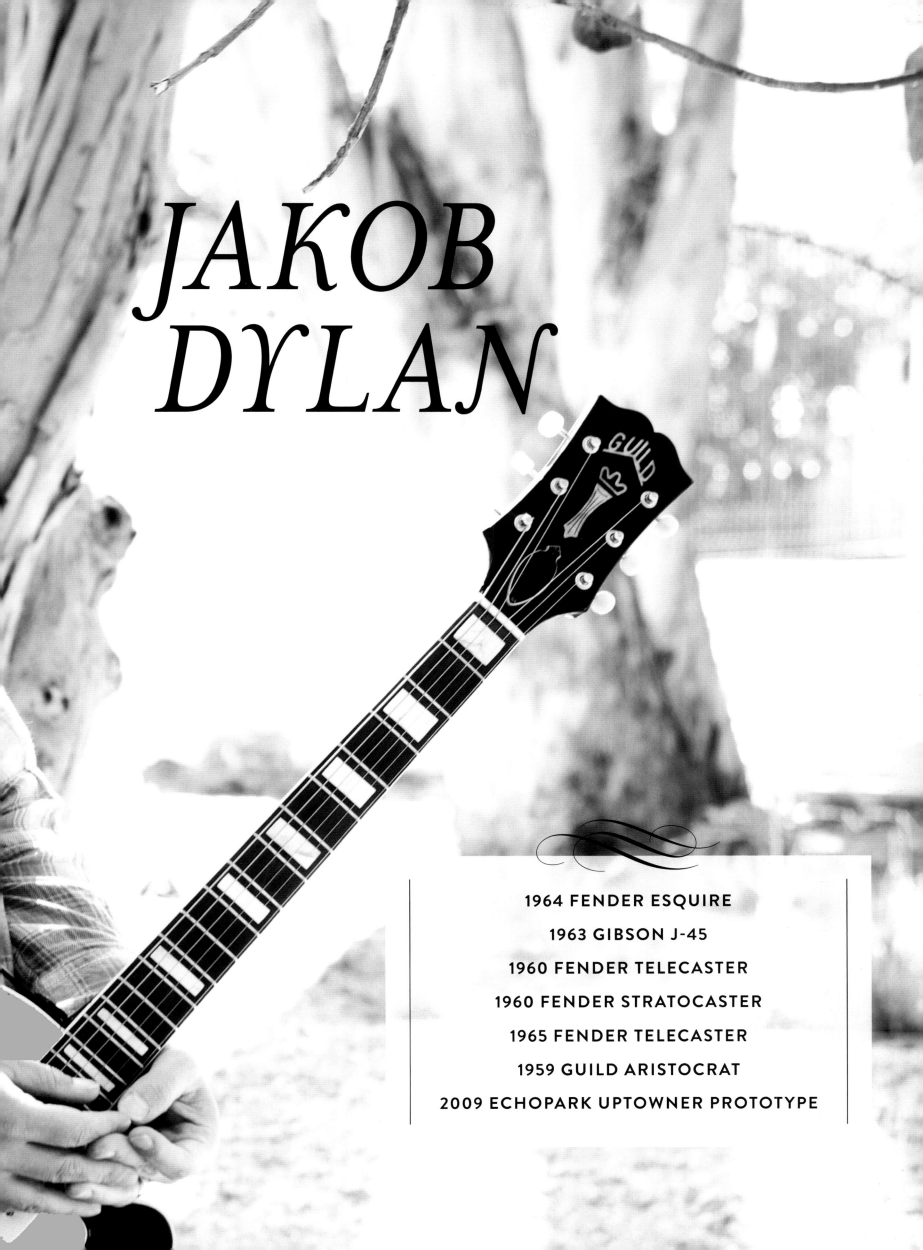

JAKOB DYLAN

1964 FENDER ESQUIRE

1963 GIBSON J-45

1960 FENDER TELECASTER

1960 FENDER STRATOCASTER

1965 FENDER TELECASTER

1959 GUILD ARISTOCRAT

2009 ECHOPARK UPTOWNER PROTOTYPE

"I'm the only guy in Malibu who doesn't surf," says Jakob

Dylan, cracking a wry smile as he surveys the Pacific Ocean from the backyard of his new home near the Malibu coastline. "I don't even go in the water. All those fish." He laughs. "Do you know what they *do* in there?"

Not that Dylan has much time to hit the beach these days. He's about to release *Glad All Over*, the first new album in seven years from his watertight rock and roll combo, the Wallflowers. Recorded at Nashville's Easy Eye studio with producer Jay Joyce (Emmylou Harris, Cage the Elephant), *Glad All Over* is a welcome return, effectively re-establishing the Wallflowers as the missing link between older classic rock outfits like Tom Petty and the Heartbreakers and younger roots-oriented bands like the Gaslight Anthem.

"I didn't play electric music for a couple of years," Dylan says, referring to 2008's *Seeing Things* and 2010's *Women + Country*, the acoustic-oriented solo albums he released during the band's long hiatus. "But I started standing back and going, 'Why am I not playing with the Wallflowers?' It's just a great group. I hear the influence of the band in new music that's out there now. That's what time does. But it's also kind of a reconfirmation that we were right when we started the group in 1990 or so."

Dylan describes the Wallflowers in their early days as "totally ambitious—and we didn't really have a plan." That youthful optimism was repeatedly put to the test throughout the band's nascent years. Members came and went. The band was dropped by its first label after its self-titled 1992 debut sold poorly, and Dylan's lineage (he's the youngest of four children born to Bob Dylan and his first wife, Sara) occasionally proved more baggage than boon. It wasn't until 1996 that the Wallflowers finally found a mass audience with the T-Bone Burnett–produced *Bringing Down the Horse*, which contained the hits "One Headlight," "The Difference," and "6th Avenue Heartache," and eventually sold more than six million copies.

The three albums that followed—2000's *(Breach)*, 2002's *Red Letter Days,* and 2005's *Rebel, Sweetheart*—were built around the band's rich, organ-stoked sound, and they met with critical raves, if not multi-Platinum sales. But by the time of *Rebel, Sweetheart*, Dylan now admits, "I think we were kind of losing the plot a little bit." It was only in the last few years, he says, that he, keyboardist Rami Jaffee, and bassist Greg Richling, his longtime bandmates in the Wallflowers, finally realized that their aim had been true all along.

"We appreciated how sturdy we were," Dylan says with a smile, clearly relishing the adjective. "If you want somebody to push the envelope all the time and be inventive, you might not think that's what we do. But my interest has always been in tradition. And to me, the possibilities within the confines of what we like in rock and roll are endless."

Dylan has a similar respect for the traditional where his guitars are concerned. Though he spent countless hours during the Eighties hanging out in Sunset Strip guitar shops, he says he "never drank the Kool-Aid on the pointy headstocks." The pure, uncluttered functionality of the Fender Telecaster has always been more his speed. "I guess my appreciation for guitars is more aesthetic than out of me being a gearhead," he reflects. "I think guitars are first and foremost tools and storytellers, and there's obviously romanticism attached to them that I felt when I was 15 and still feel today. Most things that you're really passionate about when you're a kid you'll change your mind about, or gravitate toward something else later. But guitars still turn me on like they did when I was 15."

Dylan says that he's "not a guitar snob. The idea of spending $8,000 on a guitar is silly to me, no matter how much money I have." But he still has a number of drool-worthy axes in his collection, which he was kind enough to share with *Guitar Aficionado*.

> "Guitars are first and foremost tools and storytellers, and there's obviously romanticism attached to them that I felt when I was 15 and still feel today."

Strumming an
E chord on his
workhorse J-45;
(previous page)
with his 1959
Guild Aristocrat

"The pickguard's not right. I like things
that look classic but, if you look a little closer,
there's something different."

1964
FENDER ESQUIRE

"MY FIRST GUITAR WAS A 1953 Telecaster that was gifted to me," Dylan recalls. "It was later stolen right out of my room, and it was a number of years before I wanted to get nice equipment again. But then you come around and realize that you've gotta have nice stuff; these are your tools. When we first started touring, I had three newer Telecasters that weren't very good. They kept falling apart in every way imaginable. I finally traded all three of them in for this one. I went out for years with this as my only guitar. It didn't break strings, it didn't fall apart, and I've always felt good having it. The pickguard's not right. That's the way it looked when I got it, but Fender didn't have black pickguards on the Esquires with rosewood necks. I like things that look classic but, if you look a little closer, there's something different."

1963
GIBSON J-45

Most of the songs Dylan has recorded, both with the Wallflowers and as a solo artist, were written on this now-worn Gibson acoustic. "That's the first guitar I bought for myself," he says. "I was 18, and I took all my money and bought that. I won't even say I went looking for a J-45—I like all Gibson acoustic guitars—but it's one of those guitars that has always stayed in the house, and it's always been the one that's there for me. Guitars have stories to tell: some of them have terrible stories to tell; some have great ones. This one always tells me something interesting."

1960
FENDER TELECASTER

Dylan received this gorgeous guitar several years ago as an anniversary gift from his wife, who purchased it from Norman's Rare Guitars. "This is similar to my touring one, except it looks really nice," he says with a laugh. "This one's too nice to take on tour. I've recorded a little with it, but mostly I just love looking at it."

1960
FENDER STRATOCASTER

Another sweet find from Norman's Rare Guitars, this vintage Strat came into Dylan's life more than a decade ago. "You just have a checklist of things you want. I'd always wanted an old Strat—I'd still love to have a '57 with the two-tone sunburst—and this one just stuck out to me, so I grabbed it when I had the opportunity. I played it in one of the band's videos about 10 years ago, and I recorded with it a little, but it's another one I really just enjoy looking at. It's in great shape. It's meant to be played, but it's also a real antique, something to just hold and stare at."

1965
FENDER TELECASTER

This rare sunburst-finish 1965 Tele with a maple neck was passed down to Dylan from one of his older brothers. "I played it on the band's first record and in the band's first video [*1992's 'Ashes to Ashes'*]," he says. "I had no reason to suspect that it was a rare guitar until I was getting it repaired by Andy Brauer and he called me up and asked to buy it for $2,000. I said no, and then the price jumped to $10,000 in a matter of 20 seconds. [*laughs*] And then I was led to understand how unusual it is."

1959
GUILD ARISTOCRAT

Dylan first became enamored of Guild Aristocrats after seeing a tape of Keith Richards playing one during a Rolling Stones performance on *The Ed Sullivan Show*. He finally acquired this one about five years ago. "It's hollow, so it's really light, and it's just a screamer with those P-90s. I'm surprised more people didn't play them. Buddy Miller plays them, I know, but they're not easy to come by. I think I had it out on tour for a minute on *Women + Country*, but I got nervous about traveling with it. Guitars get hit all the time on the road."

2009
ECHOPARK UPTOWNER PROTOTYPE

While Dylan's taste doesn't usually run to boutique guitars, he says he's totally fallen in love with this example built by Gabriel Currie of L.A.'s Echopark Guitars, which has quickly become his favorite for live performances. "Telecasters are noisy and twangy live, and Strats aren't always right for me, so I really wanted something more like a Gretsch or a Les Paul, but lighter in weight. So Gabriel and I talked about getting more of that Gretsch sound out of something that looked classic but unfamiliar at the same time." This hollowbody—one of the first six guitars Echopark ever produced—features a dog-eared P-90 in the bridge and a DeArmond pickup at the neck, as well as an alder body with a maple top, a center block to reduce feedback, and a neck crafted from the remains of an antique dinette set. "Gabriel's terrific," Dylan enthuses. "He's got something really special going on."

RICK NIELSEN

1955 LES PAUL

1963 FENDER TELECASTER

1974 HAMER STANDARD PROTOTYPE

1963 GUILD MERLE TRAVIS

1958 GIBSON FLYING V

1958 GIBSON EXPLORERS

1978 HAMER CHECKERBOARD STANDARD

1981 HAMER FIVE-NECK

2004 MARTIN HERRINGBONE
DREADNOUGHT "NEGATIVE"

1953 FENDER TELECASTER

1958 GIBSON LES PAUL STANDARD

The financial rewards of a 40-year career as the guitarist and primary songwriter in Cheap Trick afford Rick Nielsen the means to purchase pretty much any daily driver he desires. But the man responsible for penning such classic rock staples as "Surrender" and "I Want You to Want Me" cruises around his hometown of Rockford, Illinois, in a tiny black Smart car, albeit one with a custom-made Telecaster-shaped rearview mirror and custom chrome doorsills engraved with the names of his wife, children, and grandchildren.

As he drives toward the storage facility where Cheap Trick keep much of their old gear, Nielsen pilots the little car around town with aplomb, and given that he has lived in Rockford since he was eight years old, he could probably do so in his sleep. As we zip down the road, the guitarist points over a dilapidated fence to a grey house where he lived with his parents when he was a teenager. The dwelling is now covered with vines and in need of repair, but the garage where Cheap Trick practiced in the early Seventies, on the rare occasions when they weren't out on the road, is visible through the overgrowth.

"By the time Cheap Trick signed with Epic in '76, we were doing great," Nielsen says. "We had a Lincoln Continental with suicide doors on it, and then we had a big Cadillac Eldorado that we could all fit into. We also had our own van, and then we got a bigger truck as well as a GMC motor home.

"One of our last shows before we got our deal was with Tom Petty opening for us at a place called Beginnings in Schaumberg," he continues. "It was kind of a big club, and I think we made $10,000 that night. It was like, 'Wow!' And then we got the record deal and we went back to $250 a night."

Nielsen's father, who was a singer of devotional music and opera, moved the family from Chicago to nearby Rockford in 1956 to take over a music store called American Beauty Music House. "My uncle, George Nielsen, who worked for Muzak, was here in town, and he talked my dad into going into retail," Nielsen recalls. "So we moved out here in 1956 and we lived at a place called the Flying Saucer Motel."

Nielsen, who was an only child, spent much of his time helping out at the store. "Since both of my parents were working, I would walk to the store after school. It was feast or famine and long, long hours, and it made me realize that being in retail is not the greatest thing on earth," he says.

When the young Nielsen wasn't at the store with his father, he was often traveling with him to singing gigs. "My father was a choir director and he sang at churches and did concerts," Nielsen says. "It wasn't, like, all religious music, but it wasn't pop music—it was called 'secular music'—and they toured all over the country. By the time I was about 12 or 14, I'd been to 48 states and Mexico."

The road seemed a much better place to be than school, where the young Nielsen struggled to fit in. "If I liked the teacher, I did real good, but if I thought I was smarter than the teacher, I couldn't handle it," he says. "So the good teachers liked me and the bad teachers didn't. Back in seventh grade, I was first chair in band on both drums and flute. And one day I told the band director, 'You are an incompetent, drunken fool who doesn't deserve to teach music to me or anyone else.' I was thrown out of the Rockford school system music program for life!"

The Cheap Trick storage facility is on the edge of town. The band's equipment fills many large lockers, and while most of it still functions, the band has also kept some of the gear that was destroyed when a stage collapsed during an outdoor performance in Ottawa in 2011. The stage was labeled a possible crime scene by Canadian authorities afterward, and much of the band's gear, including Nielsen's guitars, languished outdoors in rainy weather for several days. "Our stuff got wrecked sitting out there," Nielsen laments.

Other lockers contain much happier mementos of Cheap Trick's career, such as gifts from fans, retired amplifiers, and dozens of guitars, including the ones that Nielsen keeps at the ready as his secondary touring rig. Among these are an impressive array of Gibson Custom Historic Les Pauls, a pair of Lonnie Mack–style Flying Vs, and a well-worn 1985 Strat-style DiMarzio with a single humbucking pickup and Floyd Rose tremolo that Nielsen has used steadily for decades. Also on hand is the third of the five-neck guitars that Hamer has built for him. "This has one neck that's a mandocello, which makes it a 38-string instead of a 36-string like the other two five-necks," Nielsen points out. The guitarist deploys one of the unwieldy instruments every night when the band plays "Surrender," and even though this example is fashioned from hollowed-out korina, it's astonishingly heavy. Says Nielsen, "Walk around with that for a few hours and see how your back feels!"

"I've sort of wanted to have a Cheap Trick museum ever since kids used to show up from all over the world at my parents' store to take pictures."

With his 1955 Les Paul
"Goldtop" and its original,
road-worn case; (previous page)
with a small selection of his
400-plus guitar collection

These are just a few of the guitars in Nielsen's legendary collection, which numbers more than 400. Some are one-of-a-kind custom confections, most notably his legendary checkerboard Hamer Standard and Vector guitars, and "Uncle Dick," a double-neck crafted in Nielsen's own cartoon likeness. Others are blue-chip vintage examples, like 1958, 1959, and 1960 sunburst Gibson Les Paul Standards, a pair of original Gibson Explorers, any number of mouth-watering pre-CBS Fenders, and a variety of old Gretsches. In the following pages, Nielsen tells us about some of his favorites.

From the storage facility, we head to Nielsen's home, a ranch house that he had built with a lab-yrinthine, 14-foot-deep basement that houses a movie theater, a bar, a guitar vault, amplifiers (including the Orange 2x12 combo that he used on Cheap Trick's first album), and what can only be termed "Nielsen's collection of other collections," including coins and stamps.

And then there's the Cheap Trick–related memorabilia and documentation. Nielsen has saved every boarding pass he's ever been issued (more than 5,000), almost every show contract from the band's early career, flyers, mailers, backline sketches, and even Cheap Trick poker chips from the band's 2009 Las Vegas residency. Much of this trove was displayed from August 2012 through April 2013 in a 5,000-square-foot exhibit at Rockford's Burpee Museum of Natural History. "The museum asked me if I wanted to do something, and I said, 'Sure,' as I've sort of wanted to have a Cheap Trick museum ever since kids used to show up from all over the world at my parents' store to take pictures," Nielsen says.

Most people would be thrilled to have their life and achievements celebrated in a museum exhibit, but Nielsen also seems genuinely grateful and humbled by the honor, and derives as much pleasure from the process of assembling the artifacts as from the renown that it reflects. Nielsen has had guitars and other objects displayed before at such venues as the Henry Ford Museum and the Museum of Fine Arts Boston as well as at, he says, "every Hard Rock in the world. Most of it is actually even mine!"

Cheap Trick still play more than 100 gigs a year and are showing no signs of tempering their schedule. For Nielsen, being a working guitarist in a successful rock band is a dream come true, and one that he is not ready to walk away from.

"I would always tell people I had three wishes," he says before pulling the Smart car out of his driveway and to parts unknown. "I didn't want to be the best-looking guy in the world; I got that. I didn't want to be the richest guy in the world; I got *that*. The third one, I am still working on."

"Back in Sixties, a 1955 Les Paul was just a used
guitar. There was nothing vintage about it, and it was
really something of a dog, to boot."

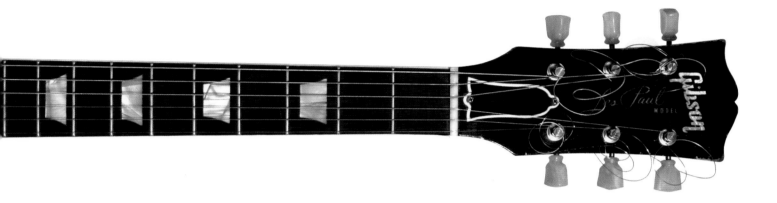

1955
LES PAUL

THIS IS MY FIRST LES PAUL. It's a '55 that I bought in the Sixties for $65. It was my main instrument for the whole time that I was in Fuse, a band that I played guitar and keyboards in before Cheap Trick. Back in Sixties, a 1955 Les Paul was just a used guitar. There was nothing vintage about it, and it was really something of a dog, to boot. You didn't see any of the guys in the English bands playing them. Keith Richards had a Les Paul with a vibrato. Brian Jones had Firebirds.

I bought this goldtop from the "A" bookstore right next to the Times Theater in my hometown of Rockford, Illinois, and proceeded to drag it all over Europe. I built a flight case for the guitar myself, and I even stenciled my name on the back of the body. I beat that thing to death. It had dents on the top from my ring hitting the top of the body. The only time I lent the guitar was when Fuse's other guitarist, Craig Myers, borrowed it. He dropped it, and the guitar snapped in the middle of the headstock. Go figure. —*RICK NIELSEN*

1963
FENDER TELECASTER

Back in 1980, Jack Douglas, who had produced Cheap Trick's first album, called our drummer, Bun E. Carlos, and me and asked us to come to New York to play on *Double Fantasy*, the record that he was working on with John Lennon. We arrived from Canada the day that my son Dax was born. My wife gave me a hall pass to not be present at his birth, and I would have missed that only for John Lennon.

One of the guitars I'd brought was my Telecaster with a Parsons/White StringBender. I remember that the only guitars John had at the studio were the three-quarter-scale Rickenbacker he had played at Shea Stadium—it still had the set list from the show taped on the side—and a crazy guitar that looked like a spaceship, the strings on which must have been 10 years old! I was like, "John, you should not be playing that. It's just wrong."

Thinking back on it, people were probably just too scared to tell John Lennon what kind of guitar he should be playing. John had never seen a Telecaster with a Parsons/White B-Bender on it, but he liked the guitar so much that I said, "Hey, I've got enough guitars; why don't you try this one and I'll come pick it up in a couple of months." I eventually got it back from Yoko, three years after he was murdered.

Sadly, the tracks that we played on for *Double Fantasy* ended up being replaced by guys who sound to me like they're playing in a lounge band. But you can hear me and Bun E. on a version of "I'm Losing You" that appears on the *John Lennon Anthology* that came out in 1998. —*R.N.*

1974
HAMER STANDARD PROTOTYPE

In 1973, I was living in Philadelphia and playing in a band called Sick Man of Europe with Tom Petersson and Bun E. Carlos, both of whom would soon end up in Cheap Trick, and Robert "Stewkey" Antoni from Todd Rundgren's late-Sixties group Nazz on vocals. We were going nowhere, we had no money, and my wife was pregnant with my first son.

I had already built up a reputation as a guy who had good guitars, which is probably why I got a call from Paul Hamer, who at the time was a mailman in Illinois. Paul wanted to buy one of my 1959 sunburst Les Pauls. I hated to sell the thing, but he wanted to pay me $2,500 for the guitar, for which I had paid about $500. So I sold it to him.

Paul took the guitar back to Illinois, sold it for even more money, and used the cash to start Northern Prairie Music, which was primarily a repair shop, in Evanston, Illinois. I moved back to Illinois as well and started Cheap Trick soon afterward. Paul and I reconnected after I brought my white 1952 Telecaster into his shop for some work.

Paul knew that, in addition to guitars, I had a lot of parts. One day, the guys at Northern Prairie said they wanted to try their hand at building a guitar and asked me what I would like. I chose the Gibson Explorer shape.

They made the guitar, which became the first Hamer. If you notice, the knobs on it are parallel to the neck, instead of at an angle like on the later ones. The bridge, tailpiece, and knobs are all real Gibson Les Paul Standard stuff, and the pickups are PAFs. The truss rod cover with the initials "JSK" was a custom job I found at some store. When people asked me about it, I'd tell them that the guitar had once belonged to John F. Kennedy's younger cousin. —R.N.

1963
GUILD MERLE TRAVIS

The first time that I saw one of these was in a magazine, in a black-and-white ad for Guild. I remember thinking, This thing is so cool! From that point on, the 1963 Guild Merle Travis was my Holy Grail. I searched for more than 30 years without even seeing one. Eventually, I figured out that only three were ever manufactured, and that brand-new they cost $2,000. That was a lot at the time. Remember, in 1963 a Strat cost something like $269. For two grand, you could buy a Ford Mustang!

After years of searching and asking everyone under the sun if they knew where I could find one—most people hadn't even heard of the guitar—I finally got George Gruhn at Gruhn Guitars in Nashville to admit that he had one. But he said it was smashed to bits: someone's wife had thrown it into a fireplace and the headstock and neck were broken off. It was in 25 pieces—a total wreck.

George emailed some pictures of it to me. I called him as soon as I got them. I said, "What do you want for it as-is? Cash!" Nobody in their right mind would do a thing like that. So he sold it to me, and then we found the original guys who had worked on the guitar in 1963 to restore it to spec. I told them to document the process, so I got 300 pictures of the whole operation. I probably spent more money repairing this guitar than I have on any of my guitars. It was major, major money.

After I got the guitar, I took it to the Aerosmith/Lenny Kravitz tour and showed it to them. I said, "You've got more money than me—but I've got this!" I took it to a John Mayer show when he was dating Jessica Simpson and said, "You've got her... but I've got this!" It's the ultimate guitar—a dream. It's got the coolest headstock, the coolest maximum ornamentation. It's the coolest coolest. —R.N.

1958
GIBSON FLYING V

Back in 1978, Cheap Trick came to New York to play at a nightclub called the Bottom Line. We had appeared at a few other places in the city already, but this gig was a big deal to us because so many big artists, like Dylan and Miles Davis, had played on the stage.

Susan Blond, our publicist at the time, brought a whole bunch of people down to the show, and Andy Warhol was one of them. I think he was intrigued by the fact that Cheap Trick were as much a piece of art as he was. We were like four aliens from the Midwest.

Andy came backstage after the show, and he was really enamored of the fact that I would play a different guitar for every song. The guitar that interested him most was this Flying V. He thought it looked amazing. You have to remember that in 1978 this guitar was only 20 years old, and unlike Les Pauls, which everyone had seen, Flying Vs were rare, and no copies or reissues of them existed. I held the guitar while we posed for a series of photos with Andy, who was smiling like crazy. While we were standing there, I said, "Hey, Andy, you might be famous, but how'd you like to have a lesson from me?" He didn't take me up on the offer, but he did invite me to his workshop.

The next day, Susan and I headed up there. We walked in, and it was like a sweatshop. There were at least 25 copies each of his Elizabeth Taylor and Mick Jagger silkscreens, stacked up and ready to go. I thought, No wonder people pay so much for these paintings. It's because they're so...rare! —R.N.

1958
GIBSON EXPLORERS

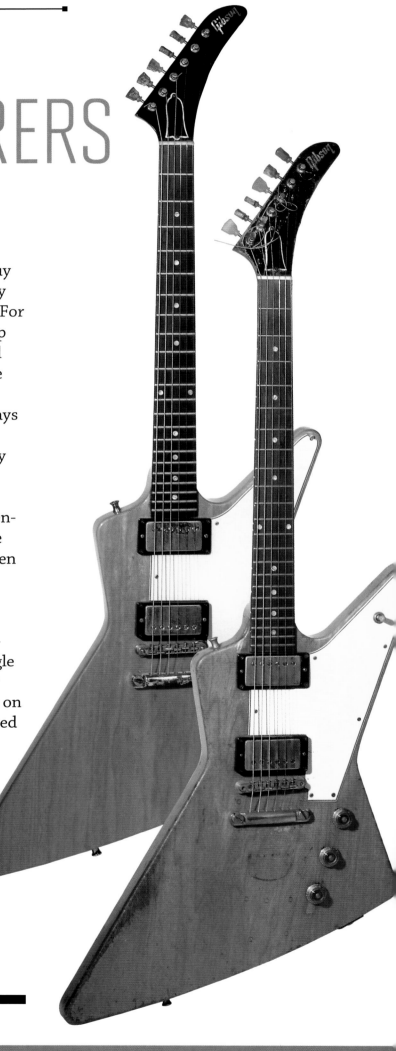

I'm a staunch believer that even very valuable guitars are meant to be played onstage. But I have to draw the line where my two 1958 Explorers are concerned; they've become too valuable for me to take on the road anymore. Gibson made only 19, and as far as I know I'm the only guy in the world who has a pair of them. Adding to their rarity and uniqueness, both have their original hardshell cases. For my insurance premiums and security requirements, I keep them (and some of my other collectibles) in a few original Gibson Collector's Vaults. Before the vaults, my insurance rates were truly astronomical.

The look, shape, style, and vibe of the Explorer has always felt the most "me" of any guitar. From the very first time that I ever saw one of these, in my minds eye, that was my look. The Les Paul, the Stratocaster, the Tele...have 'em, played 'em, love 'em, but they weren't me.

I bought the cleaner of the two Explorers in the late Seventies for $4,000 from George Gruhn. That may seem like the deal of the century, considering that, recently, one of a dozen Explorers Gibson built in 1963 from leftover Fifties bodies and necks sold at auction for $611,000. But at the time I bought this Explorer, Sixties Strats were worth only about $750, and Bursts were going for $2,000. Under the circumstances, that was a hell of a lot of money to spend on a single guitar. In 1990, I brought the Explorer to the Dallas Guitar Show, and a guy offered me $75,000 cash for it, right there on the spot. For whatever reason, even though I could have used the money and had brought the guitar there to sell it, I thought about it and said no. I'm glad I didn't do it.

As for the more beat-up Explorer, I bought it in 1981 from Larry Briggs at Strings West in Tulsa, Oklahoma. It looks the way that I got it, complete with all the dings and doweled holes on the top where a different bridge was installed. The guitar also has a neck-joint repair that you can see at the heel or if you look into the neck pickup cavity. I think Larry was asking around seven grand for the guitar, and we did a retail-to-retail trade where I gave him a couple of Stratocasters and a Firebird or two and $650. —R.N.

1978
CHECKERBOARD
HAMER STANDARD

In case any of you were wondering how beat-up a guitar would look if you played it on only one song a night but did that for 3,000 or so shows in a row, you can now consider your question answered. This is my checkerboard Hamer Standard, which you can see on the cover of Cheap Trick's 1979 *Dream Police* album. I've used it to perform the record's title track at every gig we've had since the record came out.

My fascination with the checkerboard pattern, which is pretty much my signature, began when I was a kid and the TV stations would go off the air at 10 o'clock on a Sunday night. I would sit there sometimes and just stare at the bug races or the Indian test patterns. I knew if you stared at them long enough, something good or bad was going to happen. I guess I could have gone with polka dots like Buddy Guy, but I always felt like there was too much empty space between them.

Hamer has always been cool enough to not build a checkerboard guitar without asking me first, so as far as I know there are only three of these Standards in existence. The first is the original real deal, which you see here. The second, which I recently found and purchased at a guitar show in California, was made for Paul Simon as a gift for his then very young son Harper, soon after *Dream Police* was released.

The third checkerboard Standard was built as the prize for a contest sponsored by Epic Records and the British rock magazine *Melody Maker*. Contestants had to write in and say why they deserved the guitar. The guy who won surfaced recently; he lives in Manchester and has kept the thing for more than 30 years. I told him, "I'd like to buy the guitar from you. And if I can't buy it from you, I'm going to steal it from you." He said, "I'm sorry, but I just can't. My wife and I had a special mount made for it, and it's on the wall right above our toilet."

I though that was kind of appropriate—I've been to Sir George Martin's house, and he's got the Gold record for our 1980 album, *All Shook Up*, which he produced, above *his* toilet. As you can see, Cheap Trick stuff is in great spots all around the world. —R.N.

1981
HAMER
FIVE-NECK

I have a total of three Hamer five-neck guitars, but this is the original orange one that was built for me in 1981. This guitar has been displayed in several museums and now lives on the wall at Piece, my restaurant in Chicago.

How did I come up with such a backbreaking idea for an instrument? Well, back at shows in the late Seventies and early Eighties, I used to stack up as many as five guitars for my guitar solo. I'd play one for a little bit, then throw it away and play the one hanging underneath it. Usually, the last one was the prototype Hamer [see page 139]. The other guitars in the stack were often a single-cutaway Les Paul Junior that I had put a humbucker into; my "flag" guitar, which had an interchangeable top that I would switch for whatever country we were in; and a left-handed Stratocaster with a right-handed maple neck.

Eventually, this part of the show gave birth to the idea of building a multi-necked guitar. The original concept was to have a six-neck that spun like a roulette wheel, so that I could play one neck and then rotate to the next, but then I decided to go with something more conservative—five necks in a row!

Structurally, building this monster was a bit of a chore, because I wanted a 12-string and a fretless, and one that sounded like a Stratocaster and one that sounded like a Junior. But Hamer, never to be daunted, managed to put all the ideas together and made it work. And now, because he was working at Hamer when they built it, I'll turn the floor over to Frank Untermeyer:

"Rick's out of his mind, but in a wonderful way. By 1981, we had already done some pretty wacky stuff for him and Cheap Trick, like the checkerboard Standard, an electric mandocello, and a 12-string bass, so we were used to the fact that they set all standards for going to the limit. For this guitar, we cut apart five double-cutaway Hamer Special bodies and laminated them together, and then sanded in between the necks to get that sort of swoopy look. As I recall, routing the wires through this thing was also a huge pain in the ass."

Thanks, Frank! —R.N.

2004

MARTIN HERRINGBONE DREADNOUGHT "NEGATIVE"

My father owned a music store in Rockford, Illinois. He didn't have Fender and he didn't have Gibson, but he was a Martin dealer, so I grew up with a lot of Martins around.

I had been to the Martin factory in Nazareth, Pennsylvania, with my dad once in the Sixties, right when the company was introducing its line of electric guitars. I went back again in early 2004, and Dick Boak, who does the artist relations there, took me on a tour of the factory and museum. While we were walking through the museum, we passed a display case that housed a black guitar with a white Micarta fingerboard. I stopped short and said, "Oh, man, that's the one I want! That's just totally me."

Dick replied, "Rick, we only made those guitars in 2002, and we've built as many as we're going to, but we'll make you anything else you want." So I fell down on the floor, pounded my fists, faked crying, and yelled, "I really need one. This is what I want!" Finally, Martin relented and agreed to make me the one you see here, complete with a checkerboard Rick Nielsen inlay at the 12th fret. I'm glad they did, because it's one of the best-sounding acoustics that I own! —R.N.

1953
FENDER TELECASTER

I've had this Telecaster since the mid Sixties, when a customer at my father's music store in Rockford, Illinois, traded it in for a new Martin electric guitar. I know that sounds like a crazy deal today, but you have to remember that back then, this guitar was just old, not vintage. People liked their guitars to look shiny and new, like their cars. This was last year's model—Fender had already switched to rosewood fingerboards—and the guy who brought this in probably didn't like that his maple board was getting dirty from use.

I used this Tele as one of my touring axes in Fuse, the band that I had before Cheap Trick, and also as one of my main guitars in the early days of Cheap Trick, before we got signed. It actually got stolen once in 1973, when we were playing a place called the Silver Dollar Saloon in East Lansing, Michigan. The crew was there in the afternoon setting up—and when I say "crew," I think at that time it was one guy—and somebody ran in and grabbed a Firebird III and this Telecaster. They ran out and took off in a car, and our guy chased them down the street. They panicked and threw the Firebird out the window of the car, and—get this—it didn't break! We filed a police report and the next day got a call from a pawnshop where the guy had dumped the Telecaster for $50.

I eventually lent the guitar to Cheap Trick's singer, Robin Zander, around the time that we made our *Heaven Tonight* album. I thought it would work well for him because it sounds great, looks cool—because it's white, not butterscotch—and has a small enough body profile to not get in the way of Robin's singing. I guess it worked out for him—he played this guitar on the *At Budokan* live record and for years after that. The guitar is now retired. It's still a super guitar, but it's been through the mill—and around the world 13 times! —*R.N.*

1958
GIBSON LES PAUL STANDARD

I have guitars that cost tons of money and make collectors *ooh* and *aah*, but for me, the guitar that plays like butter and looks like crap is the one you want. My 1958 Les Paul Standard illustrates this point. This guitar is one of the worst-looking flame-tops that I have or have ever seen, but it's the best-sounding guitar that I own, period, and it beats any other that I've ever played. I've used it on every record and still play it, along with several other Bursts, when we perform.

I've owned a number of these guitars over the years, and I even sold one to Jeff Beck, my favorite guitarist of all time, in 1968. I had gone to see the Jeff Beck Group (which featured Ron Wood, Rod Stewart, and Nicky Hopkins—not bad!) play in Chicago at the Kinetic Playground. After the set, I saw Beck's roadie pick up the guitar from where Jeff had set it on top of his stack of Marshalls. The guy grabbed the guitar by the body, dropped it, and the headstock snapped off. I wiggled my way backstage and told the band's road manager, "Jeff probably doesn't even know this yet, but his roadie just accidentally broke his guitar. I'm a guitar collector, so please take my number and give it to Jeff in case he needs something."

A few weeks later, I was at home and the phone rang. I picked it up and a voice said, "Hello, is this Rick? Hold on, we have Jeff Beck on the line for you." Jeff hadn't been able to find a good replacement for the guitar and needed help. So they flew me and a friend to Philadelphia with six guitars. He picked out a 1960 Burst with a Bigsby on it—a big heavy thing, as I recall—and gave me $350, which was the going rate for those at the time. And then Jeff and I stayed up late into the night and played guitar, which for me, of course, was worth more than anything. —R.N.

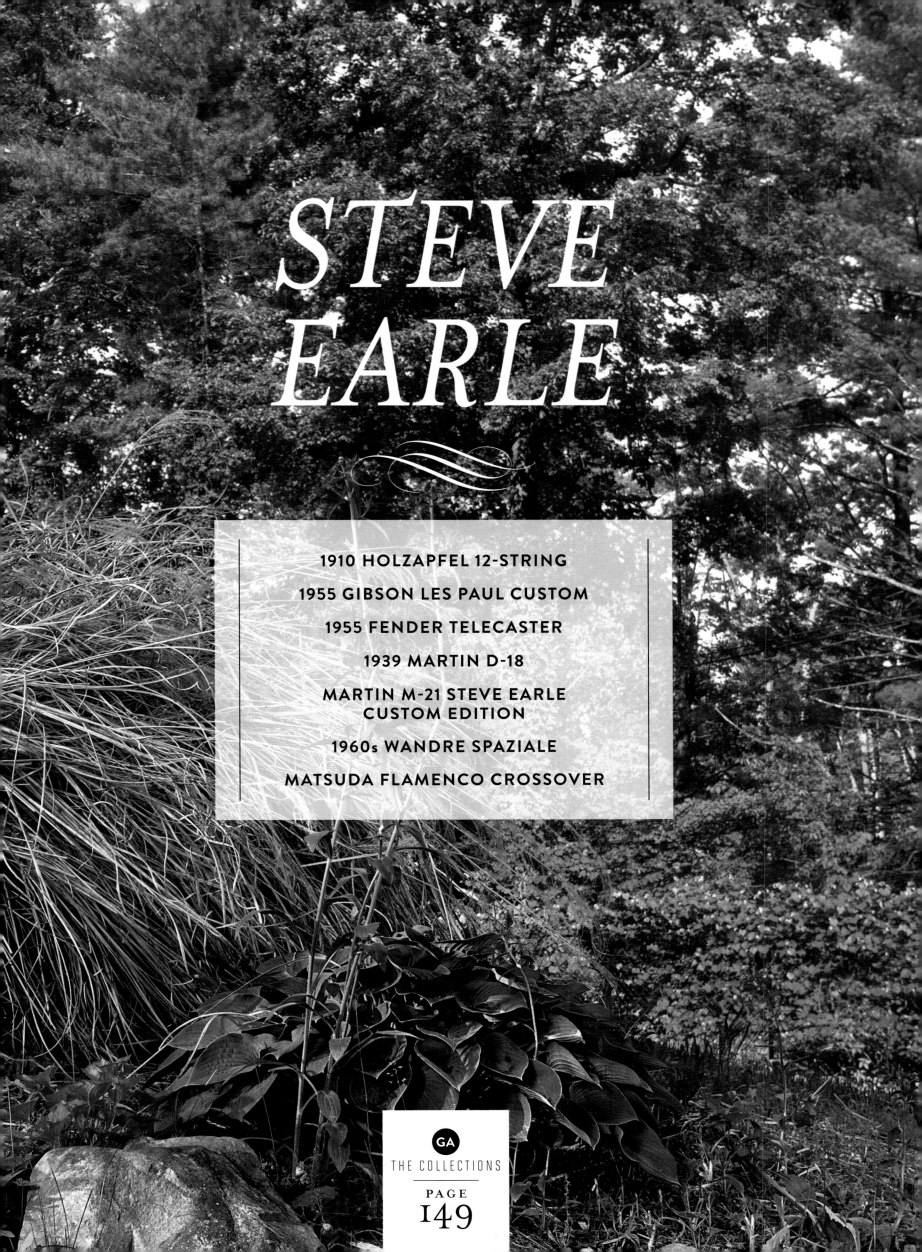

STEVE EARLE

1910 HOLZAPFEL 12-STRING

1955 GIBSON LES PAUL CUSTOM

1955 FENDER TELECASTER

1939 MARTIN D-18

MARTIN M-21 STEVE EARLE
CUSTOM EDITION

1960s WANDRE SPAZIALE

MATSUDA FLAMENCO CROSSOVER

Given the dust-bowl rasp of its owner's voice and his deep fascination with all manner of traditional American roots music, one might expect Steve Earle's Woodstock home to be a clapboard shack surrounded by rusted-out cars, or a remote mountain cabin fashioned of rough-hewn logs. But nothing could be further from the truth. The home that the 57-year-old Grammy-winning singer-songwriter, poet, novelist, activist, and now frequent actor inhabits with his wife, country artist Alison Moorer, and young son, John Henry, is a midcentury split-level on a distinctly suburban street. "This whole neighborhood was tract housing built by IBM, because there used to be a big plant up here," explains Earle, who also keeps an apartment in New York's Greenwich Village. "This was the first house that we saw when we came up here to look, and while we viewed a few others, this was the one that stuck. It had been completely gutted and remodeled by the previous owners, so we didn't have to do much before we moved in."

Afterward, however, Earle made one very significant home improvement when he converted the attached garage into a climate-controlled storage room for his ever-growing collection of classic guitars, which includes Martins, Gretsches, and Gibsons, among others. The singer, who moved to New York six years ago from Nashville, learned the hard way that the Northeast's cold winters, and the humidity-sapping radiators that accompany them, are murderous to acoustic guitars left unattended and unprotected. "The first winter after I moved to New York, a few of my guitars cracked from the heat," Earle says. "I'm kind of a communist, and I don't invest in anything but guitars, so that was like a really bad day on Wall Street for me. I lost money. My wife always says, 'How can your guitars be investments? You never sell them!' But the fact is, as soon as I'm gone, she's welcome to sell any of them."

At the moment, however, Earle is alive and well and accumulating guitars at a rapid pace. "I'm a real live collector," he says with a smile. "I became really serious about it when I moved to New York." When asked how many instruments he thinks he acquires a year, Earle admits that he's wont to lose track of his purchases. "I don't even want to think about it," he says with a groan. "I slow down every once in a while and come to my senses. I spent $110,000 on guitars the year before last. I know that much. I had a good year; other people had bad years. I've been doing, admittedly, some predatory buying. There are a lot of people dumping instruments. I'm more solvent now than I've ever been, so I have a little money to spend."

Perhaps Earle takes such pleasure in acquiring instruments because so many slipped though his fingers during the first half of his career. Although feted as a singer and songwriter, Earle struggled with heroin addiction and sold off most of his guitars to support the habit. "I had some nice pieces," he says. "I had a '58 Gretsch 6120 that was in perfect shape and still had all that leather trim around the case, the original strap with all those fake jewels on it, and the cable. I got it from a band member, and I pawned it for $100. You can't get more than $100 for a guitar in a pawnshop in Nashville, I don't care what it is. I wish I had it back. People have tried to sell to me the instruments that I lost at that time, but I basically said 'screw you' to them, because I felt like I was being taken advantage of."

These days, instead of heading to a pawnshop, the clean-and-sober Earle will typically head over to his neighborhood guitar store, the legendary Matt Umanov Guitars, on Bleecker Street in the West Village. "That's where I hang out," he says. "I don't drink, and you can only sit in your apartment and work and drink so much coffee before you start rattling apart at the seams," he says with a laugh. "But Matt is a good friend, and I trust him. I buy from him and from George Gruhn. Some people say that you are spending too much money if you buy from those places, but you know what? If I buy a vintage guitar from Matt and something goes wrong with it, he'll make it right."

It might occur to some readers that Earle is just substituting one addiction for another. While he admits there is perhaps some truth to that, he's made his peace with it. "Yeah, the guitar thing, it is a little like a drug problem," Earle says. "But I've had worse habits than this."

> "My wife always says, 'How can your guitars be investments? You never sell them!'"

(previous page) At his Woodstock refuge
with his Martin D-21 and his dog, Beau

"As long as you tune it to C or C♯, which
is what I do with heavy strings, it sounds
like a B-52 landing on the roof."

1910
HOLZAPFEL 12-STRING

"THIS IS NOW MY MAIN 12-STRING. Carl C. Holzapfel was a guitar builder from Baltimore who was alive in the early 20th century. The brass screws in the bridge are original and a peculiarity of these guitars. The only thing that's not original is that somebody contoured the neck, which is a common modification, because the necks are huge. Sadly, the guitars usually blow up when people do that to them, but this one was done in the Seventies, and as long as you tune it to C or C♯, which is what I do with heavy strings, it sounds like a B-52 landing on the roof."

1955
GIBSON LES PAUL CUSTOM

"I didn't think I would ever pay this much for an electric guitar, but I happened to get a check that made me feel like I could do it. I like it so much that I could probably sell every other electric guitar I have if I never went out on the road. This has not been touched—not one solder joint. And look at the pickups—the gold is still on them. There's not another one in this condition anywhere in the world. Normally, these things weigh 10 pounds, but this one is only eight and half. It blows my mind every time I get it out of the case—which is also original!"

1955
FENDER TELECASTER

"I was born in 1955, and I sort of inadvertently started collecting guitars made that year. Now I'm up to eight or 10 of them, including a Gibson J-50, a Martin 5-18, and the Les Paul Custom. This guitar is perfect. I bought it from Matt Umanov, but George Gruhn also had this guitar in his store in Nashville for a while. Gruhn's records indicate that the neck pickup was once rewound by Lindy Fralin, but Tom Crandall at Umanov took the guitar apart and can't find any evidence of that being true. Tom also verified that the neck, pots, and body all came out on the same day. This guitar is just the right weight and perfect in every way."

1939
MARTIN D-18

"There are very few things that are all they are cracked up to be. Mario Batali restaurants and pre-war Martins are two of them. This is a D-18, so it has mahogany back and sides. I would love to have a D-28 that had rosewood, but I'll never be able to afford that. This guitar is loud and it's clear and deceptively well balanced for a big guitar. The bridge is a nonoriginal, oversized, replacement bridge. Everything else is stock, except for one tuning key, which has a period-correct replacement. If I had to take one guitar to a desert island, it would probably be this one—in case I had a bluegrass gig!"

MARTIN M-21 STEVE EARLE CUSTOM EDITION

"The M-style guitars are the perfect size for me for live performing. The guitar will work when I'm beating the shit out of it, but I can also fingerpick on it without my arm being all the way out from my body. That's started to kill me in my old age. I worked really closely with Matt Umanov on this model, which is why his signature is on the label as well as mine. Matt somehow got fixated on the idea that the guitar should be based on the 1965 D-21 that I had purchased from him, so it features the post-war specs: rosewood fretboard, and rosewood back and sides. The top is Italian spruce."

1960s
WANDRE SPAZIALE

"These were made by an Italian sculptor, Antony Wandre Pioli, right at the height of the whole Italian design thing. He was a motorcycle freak, and the twang bars on these guitars are exactly the same part as the throttle assembly on a Ducati motorcycle. The body's plastic, and it's really just a guitar suit over a piece of aluminum that goes from the tailpiece all the way to the headstock. The pickups are floating on top of the body. They're made by a company called Davoli. Buddy Miller plays almost nothing other than Wandres and I wanted to sound like him, so I started looking for one of these. He actually plays the ones that are called Soloists and shaped sort of like Les Pauls. But I ran into a couple of these Spaziales and I fell in love with that body shape, just because it's so weird."

MATSUDA FLAMENCO CROSSOVER

"This guitar was built by a luthier from Oakland, California, named Michihiro Matsuda. The neck joint is adjustable—although you wouldn't want to just grab a screwdriver and do it yourself. That teeny brass screw is the only piece of metal that you can see anywhere on the guitar, although there may be some in the planetary tuners; they look like friction tuners, but they're not. The guitar is made with the traditional flamenco materials: the back and sides are maple, the neck is cypress, and the top is cedar. I'm generally more into stuff like Martins, which are made in a factory, but this guitar is a piece of art. No two are alike."

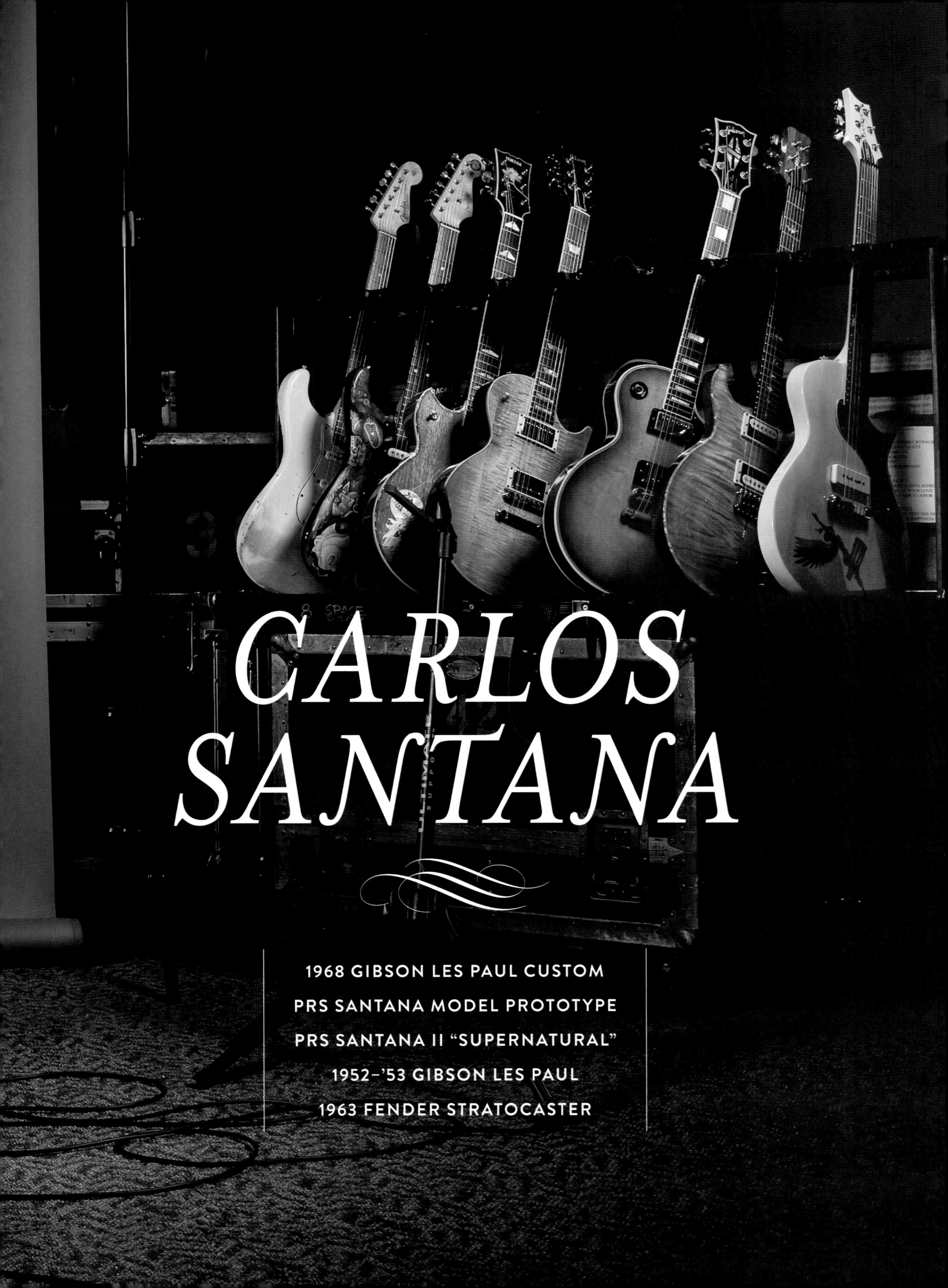

CARLOS SANTANA

1968 GIBSON LES PAUL CUSTOM

PRS SANTANA MODEL PROTOTYPE

PRS SANTANA II "SUPERNATURAL"

1952–'53 GIBSON LES PAUL

1963 FENDER STRATOCASTER

"When it comes to marriage or relationships, I'm a one-person person," says Carlos Santana, who recently married drummer Cindy Blackman after proposing to her onstage at a gig in Illinois. "But when it comes to guitars," he adds, "I'm definitely not a one-guitar person."

However, Carlos has been pretty brand-loyal over the course of his 44-year career. He was a staunch Gibson man in the years following his eponymous band's debut at Woodstock. The SG he played at that historic 1969 festival didn't last very long, but one magical Les Paul served him through Santana's classic golden period, from 1970 to 1972, when he made *Abraxas, Santana III,* and *Caravanserai.*

Carlos switched to Yamahas in the mid Seventies, designing his own model in collaboration with the Japanese guitar-making giant. But ever since the early Eighties, he has been one of the foremost advocates of Paul Reed Smith guitars. He rode a PRS to fame on his phenomenal 1999 comeback album, *Supernatural,* and on many other outstanding recordings. Smith himself will tell you that Santana can be demanding when it comes to guitars. Much like the renowned guitar maker, Carlos has a great ear and can assess a guitar's tonal virtues after playing just a few notes or chords on it.

"As soon as I hear it, I can tell if it's gonna be a lamp or something that can go onstage," he says, and laughs. "You can tell when a guitar sounds all nasal and weird. All you can do with it is wire it up for

(previous page) With a
PRS Santana SE model

a light bulb and put a lampshade on it. That's all it's good for. It may look nice, but if it doesn't have the tone I want, I'm not interested. Some people might add a lot of pedals to fix the tone, but that's not for me. It's gotta be straight from my fingers to the amplifier. If it don't sound good like that, you're not gonna fix it with a mixing board or computers."

Still, Santana isn't averse to picking up the occasional Strat or other guitar, as long as the tone is there. His collection of vintage, historic, and downright legendary guitars resides in a vault at his Northern California rehearsal space and office facility. Pulling out some of his finest instruments for *Guitar Aficionado*'s photo session, he just can't resist plugging a few into an amp and letting rip. He cues up a copy of his new album, *Guitar Heaven,* cranks it up loud and proceeds to riff over the top.

Fittingly enough, *Guitar Heaven* is an album of guitar-centric rock classics—"Whole Lotta Love," "Little Wing," "Sunshine of Your Love," "Back in Black"—done Santana style. "This is a rock album," he says. "I listen to my sound on this, and I sound like a starving, angry, horny lion. Not bad for a 63-year-old guy!"

"A guitar may look nice, but if it doesn't have the tone I want, I'm not interested."

1968
GIBSON LES PAUL CUSTOM

THIS INSTRUMENT, A REFINISHED MAPLE-TOP Les Paul, is pretty much the holy grail of Santana guitars. Carlos purchased it at Prune Music in San Francisco in 1970, shortly after his group's big breakthrough. It was a replacement for the red Gibson SG he played at Woodstock.

"That SG wouldn't stay in tune, so I destroyed it," he says. "At the time, if I wanted a new guitar, I had to ask the band, 'cause we were all paying for it. The band didn't want to get me a new guitar, so I destroyed the SG. Then I *had* to get a new one. This guitar was my main workhorse for at least seven albums. It's got the tone, the feel. You grab it and it's ready to go."

This is the guitar that generated the fiery leads on "Black Magic Woman/Gypsy Queen," "Oye Como Va," and, indeed, just about everything else on the classic *Abraxas* album from 1970, as well as the inspired discs that followed in its wake.

PRS SANTANA MODEL PROTOTYPE

Master guitar builder Paul Reed Smith began showing Santana his guitars in 1976, just as Smith was launching his business. The instrument that hooked Santana was the legendary Paul Reed Smith Golden Eagle, the first maple-top guitar Smith ever built, owned by Heart's Howard Leese. Carlos borrowed the guitar to play the leads on his 1981 *Zebop!* album and fell in love with the instrument. "It had a very rich, low, masculine tone," he recalls. It was like, 'Ooh, I've been playing a soprano, and this is a tenor.' "

Santana commissioned Smith to start building guitars for him. The guitars that Smith custom-built for Santana in the Eighties would eventually become the basis for the PRS Santana II model. The one guitar that particularly pleased Carlos was the model seen here, known in the Santana camp simply as Number Two.

PRS SANTANA II "SUPERNATURAL"

Of the many guitars that Paul Reed Smith has made for Carlos, this one holds a very special place in the guitarist's collection. It arrived just as Carlos was beginning work on *Supernatural*, which would usher in an exciting new phase of his career. Carlos has often spoken of being divinely guided in creating *Supernatural*, and the guitar's appearance seems providential.

Carlos calls it his Red Coral guitar. He knew there was something unique about it as soon as he picked it up. "It was the tonality, the weight of it, and the feel of it," he says. "And the color: a beautiful orangey, salmon red. A lot of times, the color of a guitar changes the mood for me. And what can you do without the right mood? This guitar really is supernatural. I played most of the *Supernatural* songs on it. There is the Woodstock guitar and there is the *Supernatural* guitar. Those are huge doors to walk through."

1952–'53
GIBSON LES PAUL

Another historic Les Paul in Santana's collection is this instrument that belonged to the late blues master Mike Bloomfield. "He was one of my first heroes," Carlos says. "Before I heard Eric Clapton or Jimi Hendrix, I heard Bloomfield and Elvin Bishop in the Butterfield Blues Band in 1965. So I treasure this guitar."

It was Bloomfield who gave Carlos his first shot at notoriety, inviting him onstage to jam at the Fillmore West. The event led to Santana's discovery by Fillmore owner and entrepreneur Bill Graham.

Also notable is the fact that this Les Paul was originally a gold top and was subsequently refinished with a flame top. In addition to the refinish job, the original trapeze tailpiece has been replaced with a Tune-o-matic, and humbuckers have taken the place of the original P-90s.

1963
FENDER STRATOCASTER

Carlos picked up this Strat at a Guitar Center sale a few years back. He recalls, "They told me, 'Some guy in Ukiah [*California*] had this under his bed for years.'" He bought the guitar on the spot and used it to play his interpretation of "Little Wing" on *Guitar Heaven*.

Carlos has fond memories of a recent gig at which he played this Strat through Stevie Ray Vaughan's legendary Dumble Steel String Singer amp.

"When I got this guitar, I had the same dream over and over, where Stevie Ray came to me," he says. "In the dream, Stevie Ray said, 'Listen, Carlos, you know where I am, man. I'm not in the body anymore. And where I am, I have no fingers. I'm just pure light. But I miss the sound and feel of my guitar. Please call my brother Jimmie and ask him to lend you my Steel String Singer. I need to feel your fingers through this amplifier.'

"A few nights later, I had the dream again. So I called Jimmie Vaughan and asked to borrow the amp, and he was like, 'Hell no!' But then René Martinez, who was Stevie Ray's guitar tech, had the same dream too. He called Jimmie and told him. Next thing I knew, the amp arrived.

"The amp and the Strat came in time for a gig at Madison Square Garden. I plugged the guitar into the amp at soundcheck, and it was like...*whoosssh!* I said, 'I wanna play the whole concert with this!'"

BRIAN SETZER

1959 GRETSCH 6120

LIME GOLD GRETSCH HOT ROD

1959 GRETSCH "STRAY CAT" 6120

1957–'58 GRETSCH WHITE FALCON

EMERALD-GREEN GRETSCH HOT ROD

You won't find many successful musicians forsaking Southern California's balmy climes for Minneapolis' frigid environs, but that's just what Brian Setzer did. In 2005, the guitarist relocated to the city from Los Angeles, his home for two decades. The move apparently did nothing to slow him down. Since then, the former Stray Cats frontman has recorded several outstanding albums, including the rocking solo disc *13* and his most recent studio effort with the Brian Setzer Orchestra, *Songs from Lonely Avenue*, a jazzy, sophisticated collection of self-penned material that many critics praised as some of the finest work in his 30-year career.

"Minneapolis is a good place to be," Setzer says as he relaxes among an impressive assortment of vintage and custom Gretsch guitars and classic amps scattered about his downtown loft. "It's really nice up here, if you don't mind the cold weather. The people are great, it's not crowded, and there is no rush-hour traffic. You can drive 15 minutes and go fishing or enjoy any variety of outdoor activities. There's also a really good music scene downtown."

Although Setzer spent most of 2010 enjoying the comforts of home away from the road, he didn't relax idly by the ol' fishin' hole. Instead, he recorded his first all-instrumental effort, *Setzer Goes Instru-Mental!*, which is the album longtime fans of his guitar playing have been waiting to hear. While he has offered a few tastes of his fierce guitar-playing skills on a handful of extended solos, or a rare instrumental track on his albums with the Stray Cats or the Brian Setzer Orchestra, *Setzer Goes Instru-Mental!* showcases his impressive talents and the breadth of his playing like never before. In the pantheon of instrumental guitar albums, it deserves a prominent place alongside hillbilly jazz classics by Jimmy Bryant, Hank Garland, and Joe Maphis as well as discs by modern style-fusing virtuosos like Danny Gatton and the Hellecasters.

"I didn't start off wanting to do a purely instrumental record," Setzer admits. "When I started writing songs for this record, I quickly completed six or seven songs with vocals. All of a sudden, I started fooling around with the melody chords that became the foundation for my version of 'Blue Moon of Kentucky.' I thought it sounded really cool. People don't really play that style of chord melody any more. Before I knew it, I had the whole song rearranged and redone. So I ended up abandoning the other path I was on and started going in an instrumental direction. Then the ideas started flying."

While the album features several covers, including "Blue Moon of Kentucky," the jazz standard "Cherokee," and the Gene Vincent rockabilly classic "Be-Bop-A-Lula," most of the songs are new original compositions. "Far Noir East" tips its wide-brim Borsalino to moody crime jazz, while "Earl's Breakdown" pays tribute to bluegrass legend Earl Scruggs, with Setzer pickin' and grinnin' on a five-string banjo. "Intermission" has the smooth *savoir-faire* of a Jimmy Bryant barnburner, contrasting the reverb-drenched, surf-inspired "Go-Go Godzilla" and "Hot Love."

The track "Pickpocket" showcases Setzer's signature rockabilly-infused Travis picking at its finest, while his solo performance on "Hillbilly Jazz Meltdown" will likely earn him respect from a new following of guitar connoisseurs.

When told that several of the songs on the album feature performances that are reminiscent of classic instrumental tracks by Jimmy Bryant, Hank Garland, and Les Paul, Setzer admits, "I don't really study other players. It just comes out sounding the way it does. But I am influenced by a wide variety of guitar players who make me who I am.

"All of the songs have a little taste of somebody else," he adds. "The end of 'Cherokee' sounds a little like Les Paul, and 'Be-Bop-A-Lula' is my version of that song, but if you're a guitar player you just have to play Cliff Gallup's solo, because it's so classic and good."

Speaking of classic and good, the guitars that Setzer used on the album included several choice instruments from his collection that he's rarely had the proper opportunity to record with before. "I finally got to use my 1963 D'Angelico Excel on 'Cherokee,'" he explains. "That guitar is a god. It has a Rhythm Chief pickup on it, and I plugged it straight into a 1961 Fender Twin amp. The acoustic rhythm guitar is also the D'Angelico, but I unplugged it and recorded it acoustically. If you're going to play an archtop, there's nothing that compares to a D'Angelico. The D'Angelico is the Stradivarius of the modern age. It sounds like a piano. I'm lucky to have two D'Angelico guitars: the Excel and a New Yorker."

Setzer played another iconic jazz archtop on "Lonesome Road." "I used a Stromberg Master 400 on that song," he says. "Wow! What a guitar. It has a big, beautiful sound that's unlike anything else. It's a whole different beast than the D'Angelico, but it sounds great as well."

However, for most of the album

"What I have is what I play. I've gotten rid of stuff that I don't use. It doesn't make sense to me to keep a guitar in a closet and just look at it occasionally."

(previous page)
with his circa-
1957 Gretsch
White Falcon

Setzer relied primarily on his trusty Gretsch guitars. "For the rockin' stuff, I've never been able to beat that Gretsch tone," he says. "I bought my first Gretsch 6120 when I was a kid. When I plugged it into my Bassman amp, I went, 'There it is!' That was the sound I was looking for. I've tried to improve upon that sound, and I've even tried playing through other rigs. I once tried playing a Les Paul through a Marshall, for example. But I never could beat that sound. It works for me."

To record *Setzer Goes Instru-Mental!*, Setzer initially planned to use that same iconic 1959 Gretsch 6120, which he has played on records since the beginning of the Stray Cats, plugged into his 1962 Fender Bassman amp piggybacked on a matching 2x12 cabinet. But his signature rig started giving him trouble as soon as recording got underway.

"A lot of my vintage gear broke down on me while I was using it," he says. "I played my '59 Gretsch through the '62 Bassman on the first song I recorded, but halfway through the song I realized that one of the speakers was blown. Luckily, we miked the speaker

that was still good. After that, the Gretsch started to fall apart. First a few frets slid out, and then the Bigsby broke. I guess I play my guitars pretty hard. I just said the hell with it and grabbed my new signature model Gretsch or one of my Gretsch Hot Rod guitars and used them for the rest of the record.

"It worked out because it inspired me to try different things. My tone on 'Far Noir East' is probably the best guitar tone I've ever gotten. I played my signature 6120 through the '61 Twin and a 1961 Fender Reverb unit. The sound that came out of that rig was just beautiful."

Setzer is an avid Gretsch fan who played a significant role in the company's resurrection in the late Eighties and has helped the brand maintain and grow its popularity these last three decades. Although he's collected a wide variety of vintage Gretsch guitars over the years, including several White Falcons, Silver Jets, and even a 1955 Roundup with a matching amp, he feels that the guitars Gretsch is making today are as good as they've ever been, if not better.

"Vintage Gretsch guitars need to be maintained and refurbished," he says. "You can't play a stock Gretsch from 1959. It probably won't play in tune, and the fretboard will probably be warped and pitted. You can get it refurbished, but that takes away some of its value. The new Gretsch guitars are pretty much spot on. I'm glad we've got them playing right again. When Gretsch came back in the late Eighties, they weren't doing them right. They lost their way and were making guitars with big, thick tops on them. I couldn't get them to make the guitars the way people wanted, which is how they made them in the Fifties."

Setzer credits Fender Musical Instrument Corporation, which assumed control of the production, distribution, and marketing of Gretsch in 2002, with taking the necessary steps to make the guitars the way Gretsch enthusiasts wanted them. He tells the story of how company vice president Mike Lewis put a vintage Gretsch 6120 through a CAT scanner in order to accurately replicate the distinctive trestle bracing used on that model during the late Fifties and early Sixties. "Mike wanted to do it right," Setzer says. "He figured that a CAT scan was the best way to figure out how it was done."

Setzer's guitar collection also features instruments that don't fall into the Gretsch or jazz archtop category, including a 1964 Gibson Firebird V with a Cardinal Red custom-color finish, a 1959 Guild Bluesbird, a 2003 Bigsby BY-50, and a 1956 Martin D-28. "That red Firebird plays real good," he says. "I have a lot of vintage guitars, but I don't own any Flying Vs or '59 Les Pauls. What I have is what I play. I've gotten rid of stuff that I don't use. It doesn't make sense to me to keep a guitar in a closet and just look at it occasionally."

Considering all the different musical avenues Setzer has cruised down these past few years, from recording faithful recreations of Sun Records rockabilly classics to reworking classical compositions with swing arrangements, it's hard to predict which direction he'll turn next.

"I just stay true to myself," he says. "Deep down I'm a rockabilly cat, but I jump in all these different directions, as cats will do. Looking back over the last 30 years, I'm very lucky. Not many people go that long. They burn out or just end being forgotten about. I'm very grateful."

1959
GRETSCH
6120

LIME GOLD
GRETSCH
HOT ROD

1959
GRETSCH
"STRAY CAT"
6120

**1957—'58
GRETSCH
WHITE
FALCON**

**EMERALD
GREEN
GRETSCH
HOT ROD**

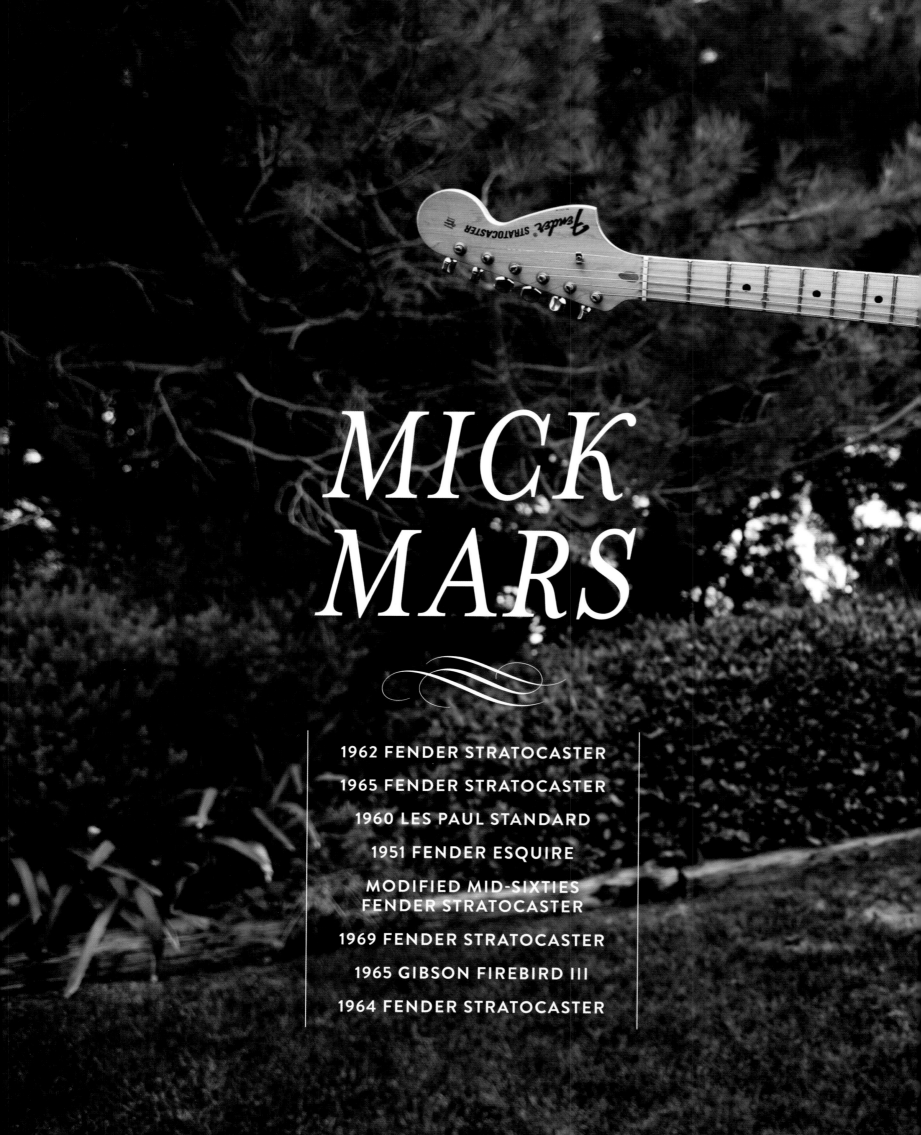

MICK MARS

1962 FENDER STRATOCASTER

1965 FENDER STRATOCASTER

1960 LES PAUL STANDARD

1951 FENDER ESQUIRE

MODIFIED MID-SIXTIES
FENDER STRATOCASTER

1969 FENDER STRATOCASTER

1965 GIBSON FIREBIRD III

1964 FENDER STRATOCASTER

The number of guitars that Mick Mars of Mötley Crüe has gone through

over the past three decades is astounding. Literally hundreds of instruments passed through his hands in the Eighties alone, from the trusty black 1972 Les Paul Custom that he used to record the band's early albums to various Kramers, Charvels, and Hamers in every imaginable shape.

"I've gone through a lot of ups and downs over the years," Mars explains. "The '72 Les Paul Custom that I used to play in the early days is now hanging in a Hard Rock Cafe somewhere in Florida. I didn't want to let go of that guitar, but I was forced to do it. I don't miss the pointy guitars. They all sounded really bad to me, and I hated all of them. They just didn't work for me. Companies kept giving me all of these different guitars to try, and I would end up trying to break them. Now they're all either kindling or I sold them off long ago."

Mars acquired a few vintage instruments during the Eighties, but he began to pursue them in earnest during the early Nineties, around the time that the band recorded its 1994 *Mötley Crüe* album with singer John Corabi.

"That's when I started playing Fender Strats," Mars says. "I owned a few vintage Stratocasters by then, and I loved how light a real Strat felt. One of the first real Strats that I ever owned was pieced together using '63, '64, and '65 parts. I bought it for $1,200 while we were on the *Girls, Girls, Girls* tour in 1987. The pickups didn't work, so I put humbuckers in it and installed a Floyd Rose. Even though it's really beat up, it's a player's guitar. I still use it onstage and in the studio."

When Mötley Crüe hit a rough patch during the late Nineties, Mars was forced to sell off many of his prized vintage guitars. Thanks to the band's recent resurgence in popularity and much more efficient (and honest) management team, he's been able to build up his collection once again. "I've slowly and carefully rebuilt my collection," he says. "I got really serious about collecting guitars again about 10 or 12 years ago. I now have about 100 guitars. I managed to keep some really cool instruments, but I like to have a lot of different things to play around with, so I'm always adding something new to my collection. I have guitars from the Fifties and Sixties as well as a few Seventies guitars. Some are really cool, and some are my player guitars. I don't have very many guitars that I don't play much. Even if I don't take a particular guitar on tour because it's too valuable and difficult to replace, it usually gets played in the studio.

"In the studio I go for a lot of different tones," he explains. "I never record an album using just one guitar and one amp. Sometimes I'll start a track with a stock Strat and do overdubs with something funky, like an old Harmony. I like to put something that sounds trashy behind something that sounds really good. That makes the track jump. I'll use just about any guitar you can imagine in the studio. It's all about what you do with the different tones and how you mix and match them."

Because Mars has remained a dedicated Strat player since the early Nineties, a considerable chunk of his collection consists of vintage Strats, mostly from the Sixties. Notable pieces include three 1962 models with black, Fiesta Red, and Olympic White finishes, a 1964 with a beautiful Shoreline Gold finish, a black 1965, a Dakota Red 1966, and an Olympic White 1969.

"I started buying stock Strats after I got that pieced-together one in '87," he says. "My earliest one is from the early Sixties. I'd love to get a Fifties Strat, but they cost too much now. At one time I had every year of Stratocaster, including a '59 and a '58 'Gloria' Strat that I really loved, but I had to let them go. I'd really love to find another 'Gloria' Strat. This lady at the Fender factory back in the Fifties named Gloria [*Fuentes*] put them together. She did the final assembly—bolting the neck on, putting the pickups in, installing the pickguard, and so on. She'd put a piece of masking tape with her name and the year the guitar was built on it in the guitar's body cavity. That 'Gloria' Strat was one of the best-sounding stock Strats I've ever owned. When I plugged it into a Marshall, it would just scream."

Mars' favorite Sixties Strats were made in the mid Sixties just after the company first increased the size of model's headstock. "Strats with the transition logo [*combining the gold lettering and black outline appearance of the earlier "spaghetti"-style logo with the thicker script of the post-1967 CBS-era logo*] and larger headstock sound better," he says, "although I personally prefer the look of the all-black CBS-era logo. I've been looking high and low for a '67 Strat for that reason.

"Sometimes I'll just run across things and go, 'I want it.' When Fender made the Eric Clapton Blackie replica, I just had to have one. John Cruz at the Fender Custom Shop makes a lot of guitars for me, and when I told him I got a Blackie, he asked if mine says 'Blackie' on it. I took a look at it and told him no, and he said

"Some are really cool, and some are my player guitars. I don't have very many guitars that I don't play much."

With his three-pickup Harmony; (previous page) with his 1969 Olympic White Stratocaster

that mine is one of the earliest ones that they made, and that it's worth more than the others. My Fiesta Red '62 is a real player. It's in great condition, but I had to have it refretted. It only had wear on the first three or four frets, but they were worn down to the wood. The previous owner must have only played open chords on it, but he played the hell out of them!"

Although the Strat remains Mars' favorite guitar, he also has a soft spot for Telecasters. Old-school Mötley Crüe fans may remember the Telecaster-shaped Kramers that Mars played on tour during the mid Eighties. "That was a transitional guitar for me," he recalls. "Nobody was playing

Teles back then, so that inspired me to play one. The problem with those Kramers is that they were really heavy. I loved the way they looked, though."

One of the most valuable guitars in Mars' collection is a stock 1951 Esquire. "I found that through a vintage guitar dealer," he says. "I traded it for several guitars that I wanted to get rid of. The dealer needed some less-expensive guitars that he could turn around and sell more quickly. I had various Seventies guitars and a few acoustics, including some older Ovations, that I wasn't using, so I traded them for the Esquire. A while later the guy called me back and asked if I was interested in

trading the Esquire for Waylon Jennings' leather-covered guitar, which he had just gotten. I tried it out, but it was so out of whack that I didn't really want it. The leather chokes off the tone."

These days, Mars may be an avowed Fender player, but he still appreciates classic Gibsons, like the Les Paul Custom he played during Mötley Crüe's early days. At one time he owned three sunburst Les Paul Standards—two 1959s and a 1960—but he currently owns just one 1960 Les Paul Standard, which was a relatively recent replacement for the ones he was forced to sell.

"It's one of the later 1960 Les Paul Standards with the metal cap knobs," he explains. "The red in the sunburst is still nice and bright. It needs to have a couple of things done to make it 100 percent original again, so I was able to get it pretty cheap. The original tuning pegs had shrunk and crumbled. The guy I bought it from replaced the tuners, but he used the wrong ones. I'm looking for some original 1960 tuning pegs for it, but I'm having a heck of a time finding the right ones. Everything else is straight on it. It's a beautiful guitar with just a little wear and tear, but it sounds and plays incredible. The other Les Paul Standards I owned didn't sound nearly as good as this one, so I didn't mind selling them, even though they were more valuable. I bought this guitar to play it."

Mars also owns a few Gibson Firebirds, including a 1965 reverse Firebird III with a standard tobacco sunburst finish and a mid-Sixties Firebird with a very rare Inverness Green finish. "The '65 is very clean," he says. "A lot of Firebirds had their headstocks broken off over the years, but this one is intact and completely stock. I love the sound of its two mini-humbucker pickups. They have a lot of character and sound differ-

ent than my other guitars."

Mars' main stage guitars are modified Strats with custom-wound 16k-ohm humbuckers made by J.M. Rolph in the neck and bridge positions, a middle single-coil, and a locking Floyd Rose tremolo. Still, he's more of a purist when it comes to vintage guitars, preferring to buy instruments in original stock condition.

"I don't mind guitars with a little wear and tear on them," he explains. "That just means that they've been played. Many vintage guitars in mint condition don't sound that great because they've never been played or they never sounded that good to begin with. A lot of great older guitars got ruined when people started replacing pickups in the Seventies. It wasn't really necessary to do that on a lot of those guitars, but guitarists didn't know any better back then. It was just the thing to do. I've had to pass on a lot of guitars that were otherwise great because the original pickups were replaced.

"If I could afford it, I'd go to Japan to buy guitars," he concludes. "The Japanese generally won't buy a guitar unless it's 100 percent original. The problem is that they're willing to pay more, so prices in Japan are too damn expensive! Some of the stuff they're selling is in such good condition that you don't even want to look at it!"

He laughs. "Sometimes it's worth paying the extra money, though. I'm having a heck of a time finding tuning pegs for my '60 Les Paul, and I probably could have saved myself a lot of trouble if I bought one that was already in original condition. But these days, a 100-percent-original sunburst Les Paul can cost anywhere from $300,000 to half a million. I'd rather buy a Ferrari for that much money. I'm a guitar nut, but to me that's way too much money!"

1962
FENDER
STRATOCASTER

"My Fiesta Red '62 is a real player. It's in great condition, but I had to have it refretted. It only had wear on the first three or four frets, but they were worn down to the wood."

1965
FENDER
STRATOCASTER

"Sometimes I'll just run across things and go, 'I want it.'"

1960
LES PAUL STANDARD

"It needs to have a couple of things done to make it 100 percent original, so I was able to get it pretty cheap."

1951
FENDER ESQUIRE

"I found it through a vintage guitar dealer," Mars says of this stock Esquire.

MODIFIED MID-SIXTIES FENDER STRATOCASTER

"[*This*] was pieced together using '63, '64 and '65 parts. I bought it for $1,200 while we were on the *Girls, Girls, Girls* tour in 1987."

1969 FENDER STRATOCASTER

In Olympic White. "Strats with the transition logo and larger headstock sound better."

1965
GIBSON
FIREBIRD III

"A lot of Firebirds had their headstocks broken off over the years, but this one is intact and completely stock."

1964
FENDER
STRATOCASTER

In Shoreline Gold. "I started buying stock Strats after I got that pieced-together one in '87."

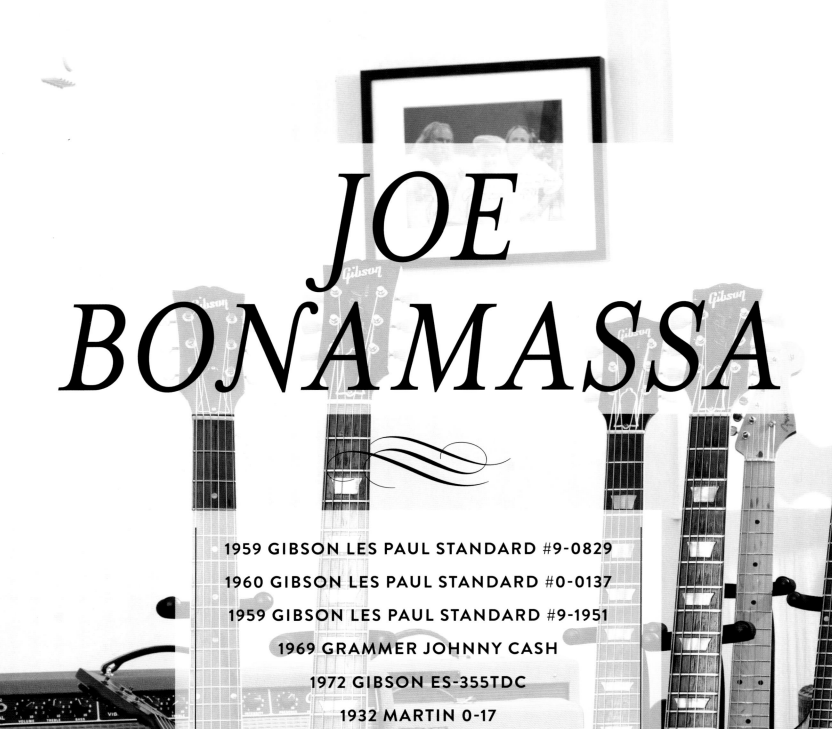

JOE BONAMASSA

1959 GIBSON LES PAUL STANDARD #9-0829

1960 GIBSON LES PAUL STANDARD #0-0137

1959 GIBSON LES PAUL STANDARD #9-1951

1969 GRAMMER JOHNNY CASH

1972 GIBSON ES-355TDC

1932 MARTIN 0-17

Joe Bonamassa isn't a man of leisure, but when he's not

touring as a solo artist or with Black Country Communion, the hard-rock supergroup led by Deep Purple vocalist and bassist Glenn Hughes, he can usually be found recharging his batteries at his oceanfront condominium in the idyllic beach town of Malibu, California. At 35, the guitarist is already a seasoned veteran, having traded licks onstage with B.B. King at the tender age of 12 and made his solo debut a decade later with the blues album *A New Day Yesterday*. Bonamassa's sonic calling card, a deft compendium of blues and blues-rock guitar styles from the Forties to the present, can be heard to excellent effect on his 13th album as a leader, *Driving Towards the Daylight*. On it, he presents some new original compositions and revisits classics by Willie Dixon, Tom Waits, and Bill Withers. "I'm really going back to the basics with this record and playing the music I've loved since I was a kid," he says.

Bonamassa was destined to be a guitar aficionado, growing up as he did behind the counter of his parents' music shop in upstate New York, Bank Place Guitars (now named, appropriately enough, Bonamassa Guitars). At 14, he received a $5,500 inheritance from his great-grandmother and used the windfall to acquire his first vintage instrument, a 1954 hard-tail Stratocaster, from a local seller. "It had a few issues as a collector's piece but certainly wasn't a bad beginner guitar. But I wasn't satisfied with just one old guitar. By my late teens I had vintage examples of all the classics: a 335, a Tele, and others," Bonamassa says, before leading us into the condo's sun-drenched interior courtyard.

As he situates himself on an outdoor couch, Bonamassa reflects on a period in the mid 2000s when his guitar buying became so frenetic that he often found himself purchasing an instrument, only to remember later that he already had one—or three—almost identical examples. "It got to be so gluttonous," he says. "I'd be on tour in a place like Japan, jet-lagged and ready to start my day at four in the morning. No Starbucks would be open, so I'd just go to the web site Gbase and throw something on the credit card. I ended up with all these guitars I didn't even play—a bunch of old Switchmasters and ES-350s and even four Trini Lopezes—guitars that were killer to look at but not useful to me on the stage or in the studio. Finally, I just said, 'Garage sale!' and got rid of a ton of stuff."

Bonamassa has pruned his collection to a mere 90 guitars, half vintage instruments and half recent models, mostly Gibson Custom Shop guitars that "sound and play killer and look just like the originals, if you saw them from row *G*." At the heart of the collection is a trio of that most desirable of solidbodies, the sunburst Les Paul Standard, comprising two 1959s and a 1960 with a 1959 neck profile. But the stable also includes less coveted pieces, such as a 1969 Grammer Johnny Cash flattop acoustic. "You've got to see this special guitar," Bonamassa says as he bolts from the

> "Guitars with good histories don't fight you. Somehow, they tend to stay in tune and play better."

A home with his 1959 Burst, serial number 9-0829; (previous page) with a portion of his collection, including, at front, his Les Paul Standards

couch and disappears into a laundry room. He returns with an old, heavily stickered case. "This one is so rare I just had to have it, even though I'm not much of an acoustic guy," he says, nimbly fingerpicking a series of ninth and 13th chords. "Now everyone who plays it wants it. It sounds incredible and just seems to have a lot of songs in it."

Another unobvious collector's piece is Bonamassa's 1972 Gibson ES-355TDC, its twin humbuckers bearing the embossed Gibson logo on their covers. The guitar hails from what many consider to be a dark period in the company's design and quality control, but Bonamassa sought it out because of its similarity to the ax played by blues legend Freddie King. "This was my first and only eBay purchase," he says. "I ended up in a pitched battle to win it for $2,900—a steal considering that these are harder to find than a '59 Les Paul or even an original korina Flying V."

Bonamassa directs us out of the courtyard and upstairs to a small room where he displays a nice cross-section of his collection: the ES-355, along with a 1961 ES-335, a 1963 Gibson Firebird I, 1953 and 1954 blackguard Fender Telecasters, a 1955 hardtail Stratocaster, a 1932 Martin 0-17, and a 1970 Martin D-41. A trio of brown cases—two Liftons and a Stone—lie on the floor, each holding one of Bonamassa's three Bursts. The guitarist tenderly unlatches each case and reveals the guitars. Their gorgeous maple tops have faded into varying shades of scarlet and amber, and they glow, as does their owner as he gazes upon them. "I could have bought a house or these three-quarter-million-dollar guitars. I chose the guitars in a heartbeat. I love them.

They're like my children," he says, with emotion.

With his Bursts at his feet, Bonamassa holds forth on the subject of originality and his philosophy as a collector. "Refrets don't bother me, but the pickup rings have gotta be right, the pickguard has gotta be right, and I've gotta open up that electronics cavity and see some vibrant original solder. I've seen some really good fakes out there, and it really bothers me. People are getting scammed by guys who steal original parts to put on fake guitars.

"I'm not a spiritual guy," he continues, "but if you buy a guitar with a scratched-out serial number, chances are it was stolen at some point, and therefore it's not good karma to play it. I find, on the other hand, that guitars with good histories don't fight you. Somehow, they tend to stay in tune and play better. So all my guitars have got to be clean and honest. Playing wear is just fine, though. Check out the worming on the back of Principal Skinner," he says, lifting his favorite Burst from its case to show where the finish has succumbed to an oversized Seventies-era belt buckle. "Honest playing wear."

The Burst triplets make an appearance on *Driving Towards the Daylight*, along with a handful of Bonamassa's other vintage guitars. A collector in the best possible sense, he sees his axes not as investments but as musical tools. "I really pared things down for the recording sessions. I only used about 20 guitars, but they were the best guitars in the world— all the best examples for sure. At one point, I looked at them and thought, If I can't get the job done with this, then I really need to stop buying guitars and just go home and practice."

"I could've bought a house or these three-quarter-million-dollar guitars. I chose the guitars in a heartbeat. I love them. They're like my children."

1959
GIBSON LES PAUL STANDARD
#9-0829

"THIS ONE'S CALLED MAGELLAN, BECAUSE it's been around the globe with me—at least where it's safe to travel with such an expensive instrument. Airline rules state that if you want to carry such an expensive guitar, you must buy a seat for it. The good news is that they will serve both a Burst and its owner a gin and tonic."

"It's got all 1959 features. I sometimes
call it Batman because of the
weird winged bridge—a one-off."

1960
GIBSON LES PAUL STANDARD
#0-0137

"I'm the third owner of this truly special Burst, which was ordered in June of 1959 and delivered in August of that year. Although the stamp indicates that it was made in 1960, it's got all 1959 features. I sometimes call it Batman because of the weird winged bridge—a one-off. And I'm honored that Gibson Custom recently recreated the guitar in exacting detail as Collector's Choice #3."

1959

GIBSON
LES PAUL
STANDARD
#9-1951

"This guitar was originally
known to the general public
as the Skinner Burst [*after
the auction house that sold it
in 2006*], but I have renamed
it Principal Skinner. Killer
in every way. This is the
most rock Les Paul I own.
Big flame equals big tone."

1969
GRAMMER
JOHNNY
CASH

"This guitar has an unusual look—a grey-burst finish—which was apparently designed to look good with Johnny Cash's black attire. It's a rare bird with an incredible tone. Everyone who plays this guitar is surprised by the sound and wants to take it home."

"This was my first and only eBay purchase. I ended up in a pitched battle to win it for $2,900—a steal considering that these are harder to find than a '59 Les Paul or even an original korina Flying V."

1972
GIBSON
ES-355TDC

"This isn't much of a collector's piece, but Freddie King played one, and so I had to have one too. It's all original, down to the embossed covers on the pickups, and extremely rare. Just try to find another from the same year."

1932
MARTIN
0-17

"This 0-17 came from my repair guy in L.A. Someone who had inherited it from her grandmother had left it in the shop and forgotten about it, so I offered to give it a second life. It's a really sweet-sounding little guitar."

JIM IRSAY

1979 DOUG IRWIN "TIGER"

1964 GIBSON SG STANDARD

1975 MARTIN D-18

SUPER BOWL MARTIN

To call Jim Irsay's multiroom office at the Indianapolis Colts' Indiana Farm

Bureau Football Center "spacious" would be a gross understatement. Even Andrew Luck, the franchise's standout quarterback, would find it challenging to fire a pass the entire length of the suite. And given how many priceless pieces of memorabilia populate the space, he'll probably never get the chance to try.

In the center of the main room, amid the wood desk and conference table and multiple high-definition TVs tuned to news and sports stations, sits the 2007 Super Bowl XLI championship trophy, flanked by American Football Conference championship trophies from 2007 and 2010. Then there's the legendary Teletype scroll on which Jack Kerouac typed the first draft of *On the Road,* which Irsay purchased at auction in 2001 for $2.43 million. Now, after touring the country, the manuscript rests in a display case along one wall, just underneath original letters written by George Washington, Thomas Jefferson, and Abraham Lincoln.

Prized possessions all, to be sure. But it's Tiger, the guitar Doug Irwin made for Jerry Garcia in the late Seventies—and the last guitar the Grateful Dead icon ever played in concert—that holds pride of place in a glass case above his desk chair. Irsay bid a winning $850,000 ($957,500 with commissions) for it in 2002 as part of a record-setting auction that also included Garcia's Wolf ax.

Irsay, you see, is a music nut. Certified. Get him going on the subject and the football business gets sacked by a wide-eyed passion. He quotes lyrics. He talks about eras and trivia, but within the context of what they mean in the greater scheme of pop culture. He riffs, verbally, like a cosmic guitar virtuoso improvising on a theme, always with purpose, but with time to circle through a few disparate ideas as he explores and refines his point.

Tiger is just one of the marquee pieces among the more than 90 vintage and special instruments he owns, including George Harrison's 1964 Gibson SG Standard, a 1968 Harptone also owned by Harrison and used on his magnificent solo album *All Things Must Pass,* and 46 Martins, one of which was Elvis Presley's and another of which dates back to the 1850s. "You can get a lyric sheet, or something from Bob Dylan or John Lennon, and they're great," Irsay says. "But the guitars are just so alive. They have so much more meaning."

"Jimmy still has that burning love for music," says Mike Wanchic, John Mellencamp's longtime guitarist and a friend of Irsay's who plays and records music with the Colts CEO at his Echo Park studios in Bloomington, Indiana. "I've never known anyone in my life who is more involved with lyrics. It's beyond impressive the amount of study he's done. He truly is a scholar of rock and roll and folk and contemporary music."

It makes you wonder if he's sure he's in the right business.

"Boy, it's really tough for me to imagine getting out there and performing...what, 300 times a year?" Irsay, whose net worth has been reported at more than $1.1 billion, says with a smile. "I think that I've always known what I can and can't do. I know what I'm suited for—but I don't let that restrict any dream pushing."

Irsay started playing music when he was young, taking up the violin at age seven and studying it "seriously" until he was 11. An ardent fan of the soul and roots music he heard on Chicago radio as a youth, he then took up guitar. "I got a really cheap Yamaha and started hacking away at it," he says. Irsay would still practice "five or six hours a day sometimes" while he was in high school and at Southern Methodist University, where he was a walk-on varsity football player. He also took classical guitar courses at SMU and learned to play mandolin in Baltimore before his father, Robert, moved the Colts to Indianapolis in 1984.

Irsay joined the family business immediately upon graduating from SMU in 1982, starting in the ticket office and moving up to general manager two years later. He took over team operations after his father suffered a stroke in 1995 and assumed ownership when Robert died two years later. But he never lost his music jones. Even now, Irsay estimates he has 100 songs he's written and recorded, but never released, at Wanchic's studio with a variety of all-star friends and hired guns.

Chris McKinney, who's now Irsay's personal guitar tech and collection archivist, met the Colts commander shortly after he assumed ownership of the team. Irsay had stopped in the music store where McKinney was working, looking for a new guitar. "He said, 'What's the best?' and I said, 'Most people would consider Martin to be the standard since they've been around since 1833,'" McKinney remembers. "He was like, 'Cool, my buddies play Martin.' Little did I know he was talking about Stephen Stills and [R.E.M.'s] Mike Mills!"

McKinney sold Irsay a Martin D-45 and shortly afterward began helping to locate and evaluate guitars and coaching Irsay's bids. "Jim is a music fan," McKinney says. "And I think, for the most part, the guitar is the instrument that drives most of the music he listens

> "I really love all historical things, but the guitars are extra special."

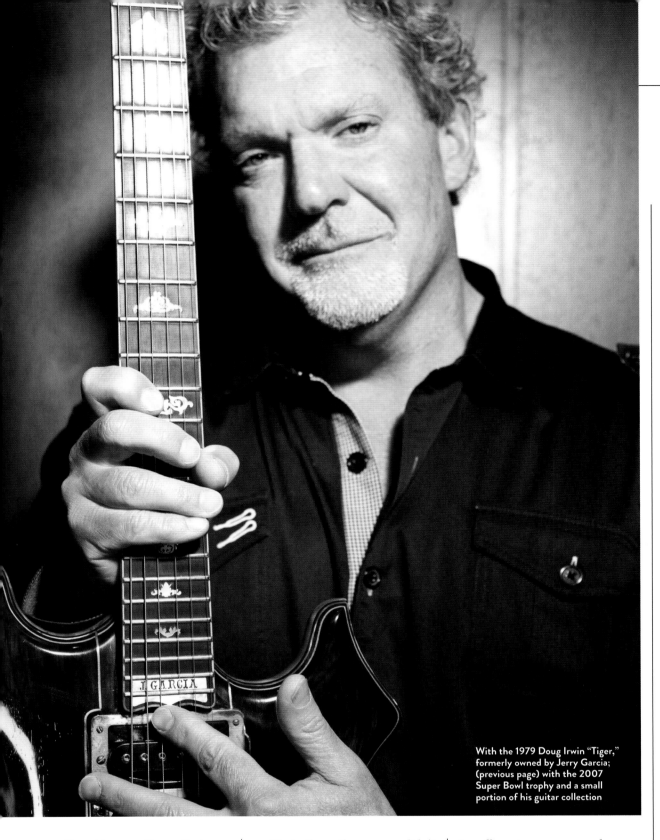

With the 1979 Doug Irwin "Tiger,"
formerly owned by Jerry Garcia;
(previous page) with the 2007
Super Bowl trophy and a small
portion of his guitar collection

ment for a Grateful Dead museum the group is contemplating.

That's something Irsay would certainly entertain. One thing he's not is a hoarder of his instruments. "Jim sees himself as the current caretaker of the guitars," McKinney says. When the wife of a Grateful Dead fan called to ask if her husband could see Tiger as a birthday present, Irsay was quick to say yes. "The guy came out thinking he was getting free T-shirts or something like that," McKinney says. "They took him back to this room, and I'm standing there with the guitar—and the guy just freaks. He was just ecstatic. He got to play Tiger."

Irsay, who has three children and three grandchildren, says he tries to maintain "a fan's perspective" with his collection. "It's something you have to continually pinch yourself about and remind yourself of. You have to continually acknowledge the privilege of being able to own these guitars and the responsibility of taking care of them and sharing them."

And Irsay—who performs a show at every Super Bowl with a band that includes Wanchic, Mills, Kenny Wayne Shepherd, and numerous others—is always thinking about ways to put the guitars to use, not only in his lifetime but also in the lives of generations to come.

"There's something energetic about pieces of history," he explains. "I really love all historical things, but like I said, the guitars are extra special. I think of the collection as continuous. Having children and grandchildren, I really get excited to think in the lineage maybe there's a player there and maybe there's someone in the later generations who will continue to grow and build it and that sort of thing. So hopefully what I'm doing is just starting something that will be around for a long, long time."

to. He said to me, 'I'm really interested in building a collection, and I want to build a good representation of the guitar in general.' So we started looking at guitars that were going to be available."

Irsay has not limited his search to celebrity guitars. But there's no denying the special place in his heart for something like the Harrison SG, which he bought for $567,500 at auction. The guitar has added value because it was also played by John Lennon, one of Irsay's musical heroes, most prominently on the White Album and in the video for "Hey Bulldog."

"Back then, those guys didn't make too much out of their guitars," Irsay says. "They either liked them or they didn't, and they would sometimes trade off and pick up each other's guitars. So when I heard it was at auction, I was just really excited about it, because, obviously, it's the Beatles, and John played it on the White Album. Yeah, that was one of the greatest purchases."

The mythic quality of Garcia's Tiger guitar was also too much for Irsay to pass up, even as the bidding escalated to record numbers. "There are pieces like that that

I really set my eyes on because they're signature pieces and such an important part of history that you can't go wrong with them," Irsay says. He was, however, alarmed when he received the guitar and found—after lighting some candles and plugging it in— that its electronics didn't work. McKinney ascertained that the nine-volt battery that operates the guitar's electric circuitry had been removed. Irwin subsequently used Tiger to record a version of Tom Petty's "Something Big" at Wanchic's studio and later showed it to Bob Weir, who solicited the instru-

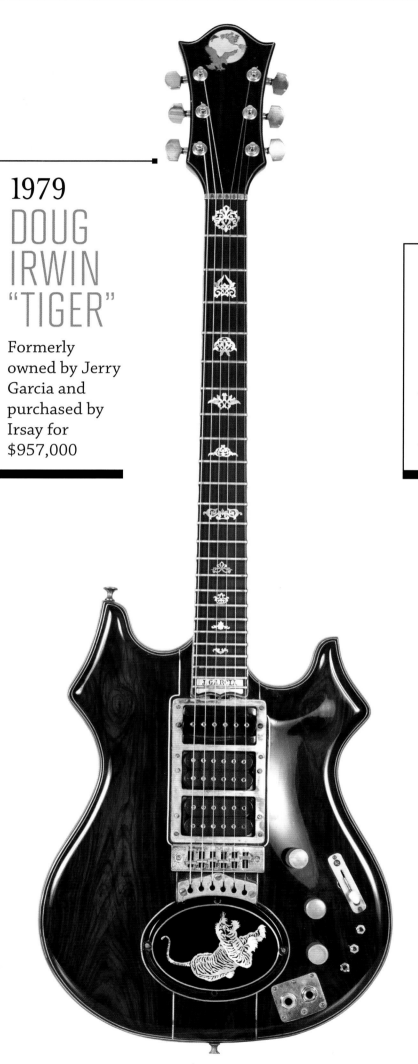

1979
DOUG IRWIN "TIGER"

Formerly owned by Jerry Garcia and purchased by Irsay for $957,000

1964
GIBSON SG STANDARD

A 1964 Gibson SG Standard previously owned and played by George Harrison

1975
MARTIN
D-18

A 1975 Martin
D-18 once owned
by Elvis Presley

SUPER
BOWL
MARTIN

A commemorative
Super Bowl Martin
that was a gift
from Stephen Stills

BRAD
WHITFORD

1959 GIBSON LES PAUL CUSTOM

1959 GIBSON LES PAUL STANDARD

2002 GIBSON DICKEY BETTS LES PAUL

1956 FENDER STRATOCASTER

1966 FENDER STRATOCASTER

Electric guitars have always proved both fascinating and inspiring to Brad Whitford. "My father had some intuition about my playing music," the Aerosmith guitarist recalls, sitting on the back porch of his gorgeous horse farm, nestled in the hills just outside of Nashville. "At first he brought home an acoustic guitar and set it by the piano we owned, but I didn't touch it. Then he bought a $25 Japanese-made Winston electric, and I couldn't put it down. Within a year I'd surpassed what my teacher could show me."

Whitford started playing gigs at 14, armed with a now long-gone Fender Jaguar and a Fender Bandmaster amplifier. Inspired by Cream, Jimi Hendrix, local Boston-area outfits like the J. Geils Band, and eventually Jimmy Page, he attended Boston's Berklee College of Music (he stayed for a mere two semesters) and developed his chops and sound. By the time he joined Aerosmith in 1971, he was plugging a 1968 Les Paul "Gold Top" with P-90 pickups into a Marshall stack and letting it fly.

Over the ensuing four decades, Whitford bought and sold more than a few instruments, and today his collection numbers around 60 or 70 pieces. "I know what I like, and that's a Les Paul or a Stratocaster plugged into a 100-watt Marshall or into a newer amp inspired by a Marshall." That would include models made by 3 Monkeys, the amp company in which Whitford is a partner. "That kind of setup has been my preference ever since I saw Jimmy Page with Led Zeppelin in 1968 at Frank Connelly's Carousel Theater in Framingham, Massachusetts."

These days, Whitford prefers to keep his vintage instruments safely stored in closets at home or at Aerosmith's Pandora's Box studio, in Massachusetts. "Years ago, after one of our overseas tours, we decided to ship everything back on a freighter,

and it went down at sea with all our gear aboard, including some nice guitars," he recalls.

Lately, Whitford hasn't had much time to commune with the guitars that he keeps at his bucolic homestead. He's been touring hard with Aerosmith in support of the band's latest album, *Music from Another Dimension!* It's their first disc since 2004's blues-roots tribute, *Honkin' on Bobo*, and it's their first album of original compositions since 2001's *Just Push Play*.

"There were times when I had doubts that we'd make another album," Whitford says, acknowledging the series of false starts and conflicts that kept the group from tracking a new disc over the years. "There were writing sessions that didn't work and trips into the studio where we just couldn't get our vibe. But about a year and a half ago, we decided we wanted to work with Jack Douglas again. Jack's so alive, and he gets *so into it*. He loves music so much, it's like it's coming through him. He knows how we work best, and the ideas started flying right

from the start."

The reunion with überproducer Douglas, who helmed the classic Seventies Aerosmith discs *Get Your Wings*, *Toys in the Attic*, *Rocks*, and *Draw the Line*, was part of the group's campaign to get back to its career-defining sound. The album's first single, "Legendary Child," blows in on the kind of sirocco riff that originally put the band on the map. Tracks like "Oh Yeah" and "Lover Alot" keep kicking up dust and tap into the vein of down-and-dirty rock and roll that all five members share as their first and deepest bond.

Not surprisingly, at this point in his career, Whitford needs to feel a similarly deep connection with an instrument in order to deem it worth keeping. "A guitar has to be fun to play," he says. "Otherwise it's just firewood. I've got a bunch of firewood I've been selling off lately on eBay. People say, 'You're selling guitars on eBay?' But that's where you sell guitars these days."

Over the next few pages, Whitford shares some of the keepers in his top-flight collection.

"A guitar has to be fun to play.
Otherwise it's just firewood."

At home with his Burst and other guitars
from his collection; (previous page) with
his 1956 Fender Telecaster

"The frets are so tiny, you have to adapt your style
to the neck. Once you get the hang of it, though,
this guitar is so much fun to play."

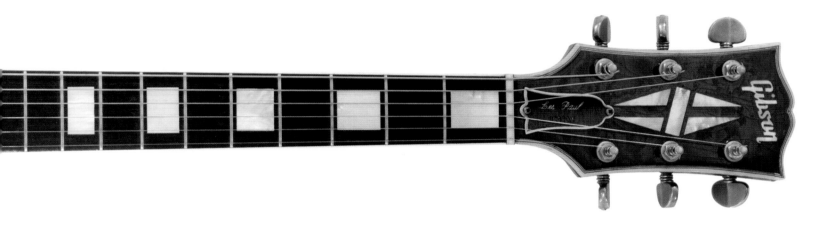

1959
GIBSON LES PAUL CUSTOM

GIBSON HAD BEEN MAKING THE Les Paul Custom, a.k.a. Black Beauty, for three years before first building the three-pickup version in 1957. Whitford's example rolled out of the company's original factory in Kalamazoo, Michigan, two years later. "That middle pickup takes a little getting used to: you can't really dig into the strings," Whitford says. "But it's worth it. In the middle toggle-switch position, the middle and bridge pickups are activated, and that makes a really ballsy sound that I love in the studio."

Whitford's 1959 model has some slight dings on its body but is otherwise in great shape and has the original frets. "Gibson used to advertise the Custom as the Fretless Wonder back in the Fifties, and the small frets take some getting used to," he says. "They're so tiny, you have to adapt your style to the neck. Once you get the hang of it, though, this guitar is so much fun to play."

1959
GIBSON LES PAUL STANDARD

"Let me play the Holy Grail," Whitford says as he grabs his exceptionally attractive 1959 Standard. He plugs the ax into a nearby Fender Deluxe amp that he opens up generously. The instrument's sonic architecture is gorgeous: burning lows, lush mids, and ringing high notes.

Whitford acquired the guitar when Aerosmith were recording at New York City's Avatar Studios, in the mid Nineties. A Les Paul collector phoned to ask if he could see Whitford and Joe Perry's vintage Les Pauls, but both guitarists had sold theirs during Aerosmith's low years.

"He felt bad for us, so he sent the guitar dealer Perry Margouleff over with five 1959s from his personal collection," Whitford explains. "Perry said, 'You guys each pick out one, and I will give you a great deal.' At the time they were probably worth around $90,000 to $100,000, and he gave us each guitar for $20,000. That was impossible to pass up."

2002
GIBSON DICKEY BETTS LES PAUL

Whitford found this elusive Gibson signature model on the wall at Norman's Rare Guitars in Tarzana, California, one afternoon in July 2012. "I thought it was pretty cool, but I left it there," he says. "A few hours later I ran into Joe Bonamassa, on whose record I played, and when I told him about it, his eyes popped out of his head. He briefed me about the guitar and how rare it was. So I immediately called Norm and said, 'I think I want to get that Dickey Betts guitar.' As it turns out, it's one of the nicest-sounding *and* -playing Les Pauls I've ever encountered.

"I've always had a thing for Gold Tops," he adds. "My first vintage Les Paul was a '57 Gold Top with a Bigsby. I had to sell it, unfortunately. It was an amazing guitar that I used on a lot of Aerosmith studio tracks."

1956
FENDER
STRATOCASTER

This road-worn Strat has accompanied Whitford on numerous tours with Aerosmith, but most of its battle scars were already there when he acquired it years ago. "I don't know this guitar's story before it came into my hands, but it looked like it was already infused with somebody's soul," he says. "It's super light and has an amazing feel, and it's a great example of a mid-Fifties Strat."

Whitford would know. His extensive collection of Strats from that era includes three from 1954, the model's debut year. "They're iconic. Nothing feels and sounds like these guitars from that period of '54 to '56," he says. "You can explain it to people, but until you hold one in your hands and play it yourself, you don't really connect with how great these guitars are."

1966
FENDER
STRATOCASTER

A 1966 model would be among the lesser-valued Fenders in Whitford's quiver of Strats and Teles, but this Ivory beauty is a rare find, thanks to the elegant binding that surrounds its fretboard. "I haven't found the definitive number they made, but I believe it's around 55," Whitford says. "I'm not sure what the story is or why they made so few. I know Jeff Beck and Ry Cooder both have one. Those are the only others Strats with binding I've ever seen. Of course, it plays every bit as good as it looks."

The guitar was a gift from Whitford's wife, Karen, and was purchased from Perry Margouleff as well. "Whenever my wife wanted to buy me a guitar, she would call Perry up, and he'd say, 'Oh, I think I have something that might be right.'"

JAMES HETFIELD

1958 LES PAUL STANDARD

1959 LES PAUL STANDARD

1960 LES PAUL STANDARD

1959 LES PAUL STANDARD

"I believe that old cars have a soul," Metallica frontman James Hetfield says. While playing guitar and singing may be his profession, creating kustom cars has become his obsession of late. Hetfield has designed and built more than a dozen award-winning kustom rides, and when he's not on the road with his band, he's likely cruising the streets around the San Francisco Bay Area in one of his cool creations. "I love to find cars that are just sitting there rotting away and give them a second chance in life," Hetfield says. "That ties in a lot to how I feel about my life. I got abused and left on my own, then I was taken in and revamped."

Hetfield's collection is impressive not only for the visionary designs of his fleet but also because many of his kustom cars are built from rare, sought-after classics. Standouts include a 1953 Buick Skylark, which many vintage car enthusiasts consider one of the most desirable classics ever made, and a 1936 Auburn Boattail Speedster. Mint original-condition examples of the latter can sell for a quarter- to a half-million dollars at car auctions, but Hetfield got his Auburn from a different type of auction: eBay. Many of his cars are initially made for show, but over time most of them get transformed into daily drivers.

Although Hetfield became a full-blown motorhead somewhat late in life, his love affair with cars started early, thanks to his older brothers, who during the Seventies introduced him to the high-powered thrills of muscle cars. The first car that Hetfield "did doughnuts in" was his mom's 1972 Dodge Charger, and he often borrowed his brother's 1967 Plymouth Barracuda three-speed fastback. "Back then, even family cars were muscle cars," he reminisces.

Hetfield's interest in vehicles went into hibernation shortly after he formed Metallica. "I didn't care too much about cars at first, because I was always on tour and I didn't need to have my own set of wheels," he says. "When the band started doing pretty good and I was able to afford a place with a garage, I got myself a '55 Chevy and built it up. I was into fast muscle cars for a while, but then I entered the world of Kustom Kulture, where you modify your vehicle to make it the coolest it can be. It's like making your own concept car, taking the best of all the cars you like and then cutting and welding all the different parts to make it all your own."

Graphic and tattoo artist Dennis McPhail, who designed band T-shirts and tattoos for members of Metallica, helped bring Hetfield into the world of Kustom Kulture by introducing him to the Beatniks of Koolsville car club. After hanging around with McPhail and the Beatniks for a while, the guitarist bought a 1923 T-bucket roadster (which he can be seen driving in the Metallica documentary *Metallica: Some Kind of Monster*) from McPhail and eventually worked his way into the club.

"The Beatniks are a cool group of guys who have been there and done that," Hetfield says. "They're some of the elders of the kustom car clubs around here. I got into kustom cars just by hanging around with them. The kustom car is what it's all about—making a prototype that's unique to you and your style. I loved that it was all about driving something old. I was never into the most cutting-edge new vehicles. It's the same with clothes and guitars. Vintage is just better, in my opinion."

Fellow Beatnik and vehicle stylist Rick Dore of Rick Dore Kustoms has helped Hetfield put together several of his most impressive show cars, including the Skyscraper (a 1953 Buick Skylark), Slow Burn (1936 Auburn), and Crimson Ghost (1937 Ford). "Rick is an absolute artist," Hetfield says. "He knows a lot about the cars—what flows and what vibes well. He knows all of the old tricks that they used to use in the Fifties and what parts are interchangeable and only need minor modifications. Guys like Rick rarely ever measure anything. They'll use their eye and heart instead, and they'll try different things just to see what's going to happen. It's an art form."

The Skyscraper was Hetfield and Dore's first project together. "The '53 Skylark is like the ultimate Fifties car, in my eyes," Hetfield says. "It was a major signpost in the development of the automobile, like the 1936 Ford. It also was an anniversary car for Buick, and they didn't make a whole lot of them. My goal was to make history by making the coolest-looking Skylark out there. The Skyscraper looks radical, but it's somewhat of a mild customization, which are the customs I appreciate most."

Hetfield also likes the recycling aspect of customization. One of his most green cars, literally speaking, is a 1952 Oldsmobile that he named the Grinch. Hetfield found the Oldsmobile rotting away in a barn in Arkansas, and he hired Robert Roling of Kustoms Royale in Little Rock to do a mild customization with it. Roling added several musical accents to the car, including a vintage Shure microphone shift knob, an old Ludwig

> "I was never into the most cutting-edge new vehicles. It's the same with clothes and guitars. Vintage is just better, in my opinion."

Speed King kick drum pedal for the accelerator and guitar knobs for the dashboard controls.

"The Grinch has a music theme, which makes sense to me," Hetfield says. "Robert and I had the same vision for that car. It's my daily driver and my favorite car to drive around. The green color is super cool, and I love the white interior, which is insanity because I have kids, but I don't care, because it's meant to be driven and used. I like to think that the soul of that car is smiling because I took it out of decay and it's now used to drive my kids to school."

Other cars that he routinely takes for a spin include a 1936 Ford that was one of his first personal projects ("I did a lot of welding work on that myself," he says) and a 1956 Ford F100 truck named Straight Edge, both of which have been worked on extensively by Scott Mugford of Blue Collar Customs in Sacramento. Mugford originally made the Straight Edge into an award-winning show car, adding a Chrysler grille, slanted quad headlights, and the tailgate and rear quarters from a 1957 Ford Ranchero, as well as fabricating dozens of custom stainless-steel parts, but recently it was transformed to a daily driver.

"Scott has done a lot of really cool rat rods, which are mainly Thirties Fords," Hetfield says. "They're super dangerous and really radical. They're like the original hot rods, but on steroids. The engines are scary; they're slammed down so the flywheel is only two inches from the ground. The transmission is right next to you, and they have chicken wire for floorboards."

Most of the cars that Hetfield has acquired recently are from the Thirties. In addition to his Slow Burn and Crimson Ghost show cars and his 1936 Ford daily driver, he owns a 1936 Dodge convertible, a 1939 Lincoln Zephyr, and several other Thirties cars. "I've

With a bevy of Flying Vs: (top row, from left) a white 1980, a natural 1975, a black 1983 '58 reissue (holding), a cherry-red 1967, a natural 1978, and a black 1975; (bottom row, from left) a white circa-1982 Korina, a natural 1975, and a cherry 1982 (also shown on the previous page with his 1936 Nash coupe)

been going backward in time," he explains. "I went from the Sixties to Fifties cars like the Skyscraper, Grinch, Straight Edge, and 1950 Oldsmobile fastback. Then I got into the Forties, and the Thirties are really where I'm at right now. Cars from the Thirties are extremely cool. I just got a 1936 Nash that's painted black and has suicide doors. It's an Al Capone gangster-style car. I really want to put a machine gun in it, but that's not a great idea. I'm working on a 1937 Lincoln Zephyr four-door sedan as well."

Hetfield owns a couple of buildings close to where he lives that provide plenty of room for him to store and work on his cars. There he also keeps an assortment of vintage amps and guitars—including several original Gibson Les Paul Standards and probably the largest assortment of late-Sixties and early Seventies Gibson Flying Vs owned by a single collector—for when he wants a break from wrenching and welding.

He admits that the garages are located just far enough from his home to keep him from spend-

ing all of his free time there, but he also concedes that maintaining his cars can be a full-time responsibility. Even so, Hetfield says, his collection is far from complete. "I have ideas for the next five cars I want to do, but to do a car properly takes at least a year," he notes. "Trying to do a car that hasn't been done before and still make it look period correct or at least make it look like it belongs from that time is a challenge, but it can be done. I can't tell you what I'm going to do next, but I can tell you that I am going to be doing a lot more."

1958
LES PAUL STANDARD

1959
LES PAUL STANDARD

Hetfield's original Les Paul Standards with his "Skyscraper" 1953 Buick Skylark

1960
LES PAUL STANDARD

1959
LES PAUL STANDARD

LYNN WHEELWRIGHT

CHARLIE CHRISTIAN GIBSON ES-250

1937 LES PAUL GIBSON L-7

1932 ALVINO REY RO-PAT-IN ELECTRO

CIRCA 1943–'44 SPEEDY WEST LAP STEEL

The guitar collection of Lynn Wheelwright is vast, fascinating, and unlike any other in the world. Although he's a member of the baby-boom generation, Wheelwright could not care less about 1959 Bursts, pre-war Martins or 1954 Strats. He finds it incredibly boring to chase after the same stuff all the other collectors covet. Besides, he's been there, done that. Wheelwright was dealing vintage, midcentury guitars back in the days when garage-sale gold was thick on the ground.

"Back in the Seventies and Eighties, that crap was easy to find," he says dismissively. "I don't know how many pre-CBS Strats I bought for 50 dollars."

In the mid Eighties, Wheelwright turned his attention to instruments from the birth of the electric guitar in the Thirties and Forties. Since then, he has become one of the foremost experts and collectors in this field. "In one lifetime, the electric guitar goes from being a joke to being the most important musical instrument on the planet," he marvels. "That's just amazing."

While Wheelwright's focus is the early electric period, his collection goes as far back as his 1793 Fabricatore. He's intrigued by prehistory, firsts, originators, and their creations. But he also has a special place in his heart for the instruments owned and played by guitar greats. Among the treasures in his large cache of instruments is the only known extant guitar owned and played by jazz legend Charlie Christian—an important piece of musical history if ever there were one. Historic guitars from the Wheelwright collection have been exhibited in numerous museums, including the Experience Music Project in Seattle; the National Music Museum in Vermillion, South Dakota; the

Museum of Making Music in Carlsbad, California; the Musical Instrument Museum in Phoenix, Arizona; and the Fullerton Museum in Fullerton, California.

A rugged Vietnam vet who lives in the snowy wilds of Utah, Wheelwright has worked at everything from construction to bounty hunting. But most of all, he has the heart, soul, obsessive mind, keen eye, horse-trader savvy, and endearingly irascible, eccentric temperament of a true collector. He played a little guitar back in the Sixties and started building his own guitars in the Seventies. From there, he segued into dealing vintage guitars.

"I didn't have a shop; I was a road guy," Wheelwright says. "I'd go around to pawn shops, flea markets, yard sales... I had contacts who bought expensive crap, and I'd call them when I found something."

In the mid Eighties, he was introduced to Alvino Rey, the guitarist and bandleader who was a major pioneer of the early electric guitar. Rey wanted Wheelwright to evaluate, and ultimately sell, some of the instruments in his own large collection.

"He started pulling out crazy stuff from under the stairs," Wheelwright says. "Like Vivi-Tone guitars, two flat-head 1929 Gibson

banjos, and wild custom-color Fender stuff, like a 1960 Tele in Lake Placid Blue and a Sherwood Metallic Green '62 Bass VI."

Among the most significant finds under Rey's staircase was one of the earliest known Gibson electric Hawaiian guitar prototypes, which Wheelwright sold to the EMP museum for six figures. Another well-known vintage dealer, who shall remain nameless, had earlier passed on the instrument, dismissing it as junk.

Wheelwright's association with Rey led him deep into the history of early electrics. As a result, he can spot things that no one else can. Like an archeologist, he takes early electric instruments apart and pores over their inner workings, looking for clues to the thought processes and methods of the electric guitar's originators. One of his most significant finds is a crudely wrought lap-steel guitar-and-amp set from 1942 that rep-

resents the earliest known collaboration between Leo Fender and Doc Kauffman, predating both K&F and Fender Electric Instruments by several years. Wheelwright found that one on eBay.

But it isn't only his eagle eye that enables him to make these finds. He's also an absolute research demon, as doggedly relentless as Stalin's KGB and even more obsessive over details. He obtained a copy of Gibson's shipping records at a time when nobody but Gibson had access to that information, spending four days, and hundreds of dollars, at a Kinko's near Gibson's Nashville HQ, where he photocopied thousands of pages.

"That was like the holy grail— the key to information," Wheelwright says. He quickly hired someone to enter the information into an easily searchable electronic database. The effort and expense paid off in spades when

"I sold piles of Teles, Strats, Les Pauls, dot-neck 335s, and Super 400s that I'd picked up over the years. And I spent all the money from that buying stuff that nobody cared about."

With a 1936 National electric; (previous page) at home holding a circa-1937 Gibson double-neck lap-steel prototype built for Alvino Rey

the shipping records enabled him to find, among many other treasures, the Charlie Christian guitar. Christian is another of Wheelwright's obsessions. Wheelwright had long been collecting Gibson ES-250s, the model that Christian is known for playing. So when he saw a circa-1940 ES-250 advertised for sale in a guitar magazine, his interest was piqued.

"I called the dealer and asked, 'Can you tell me the serial number?'" Wheelwright recounts. "The guy looks at the guitar and says the serial number is 96-039. But that's not a serial number for a 250. So the dealer goes out in the sunlight

and takes another look, and the serial number is actually 96-030. A 9 and a 0 on the old stamps look the same. So I go to the shipping records and find, 'April 19, 1940, ES-250 96-030, Chas. Christian.' The guitar had been shipped directly to Charlie on the road with the Benny Goodman Orchestra. If he hadn't been on the road, it would have been shipped to a music store for him to pick up and his name wouldn't have appeared on the records." By carefully matching the guitar's wood-grain patterns and other key details with archival photos of Christian, Wheelwright was able to identify

it as the one that belonged to the legendary guitarist.

Wheelwright got out of the vintage trade in the mid Nineties when it became a big business and, in his view, lost its soul. "They might as well be selling meat on hooks," he says. "The last time I sold a pile of vintage stuff for money was in '96 or '97 at the Dallas guitar show. I sold piles of Teles, Strats, Les Pauls, dot-neck 335s, and Super 400s that I'd picked up over the years. And I spent all the money from that buying stuff that nobody cared about—odd Gibson lap steels and crazy early electric stuff.

And by then, people knew that I was buying this kind of stuff, so sometimes I would have to pay a little more than they might have normally sold it for.

"But I tried to keep an intensely low profile. I didn't want people jacking up the price or deciding that it was cool and they wanted to collect the stuff."

By now, though, the cat is completely out of the bag, and Wheelwright has come to hold a special place of notoriety among vintage dealers. "I got to be known as the guy who, if he calls you, be careful what you sell him. If he wants it, it must be something important."

CHARLIE CHRISTIAN GIBSON ES-250

The venerable institution of the electric guitar solo might not exist today had it not been for the pioneering work of Charlie Christian. The instrument shown here is the only known extant guitar verifiably owned and played by the jazz legend. Christian acquired the guitar in April 1940 and played it until his death in 1942, notably on sessions with the Benny Goodman Sextet, an ensemble that also featured Count Basie and Lionel Hampton.

The guitar has several unique features. For example, the Gibson logo on the headstock sits atop the two uppermost tuning machine ferrules. In addition, the guitar has been refinished, and its original pressed-plywood back has been replaced by a two-piece carved back. "It was obviously a Gibson factory job," he says. "I could tell the back wasn't taken off another guitar." Wheelwright thinks the refurbishing took place after Christian's death. "But still," he says, "this is Charlie's guitar. I've never played it. I'm not worthy."

1937

LES PAUL GIBSON L-7

This sunburst 1937 Gibson L-7 belonged to Les Paul, who sent it to Gibson circa 1941 to be fitted with a seven-inch diagonal pickup that is a P-90 precursor. This makes the guitar, in effect, a prototype of the Gibson ES-300. Figuring this out was one of Wheelwright's greatest pieces of detective work. He first spotted the instrument in the mid Nineties at the Dallas Guitar Show. "I was intrigued, because every other ES guitar with a long, diagonal pickup is blond," he says.

Wheelwright didn't purchase the guitar until the mid 2000s. "As soon as I got it home, I took it apart," he says. "I'm looking at the pickup going, 'Holy crap, this isn't normal.' The U bracket that holds the pickup had been put in a vice and bent. It wasn't pressed with a form. The pickup is built different underneath and the screws are weird. I said to myself, Wow, is this some prototype thing that Gibson mocked up for Les to try?" This hypothesis was subsequently confirmed in an interview that author Robb Lawrence conducted with Paul.

1932
ALVINO REY RO-PAT-IN ELECTRO

Wheelwright had a close relationship with electric guitar innovator Alvino Rey during the last two decades of the guitarist's life. Rey was among the first champions of the electric guitar and arguably the biggest celebrity to embrace the instrument at this early juncture. In October 1932, he became the owner of one of the first 13 Ro-Pat-In Electros ever shipped. The aluminum, frying pan–shaped Electro is generally regarded as the first commercially produced electric guitar. Ro-Pat-In would, of course, later become Rickenbacker. Later production runs of this 25-inch-scale-length guitar bore the model number A25 to distinguish it from the 22-inch-scale-length A22, which came later.

Rey got tired of people remarking on the guitar's unusual appearance, and around 1933, he affixed the back and sides of a Columbia parlor guitar to the instrument. This is the instrument that introduced many American radio listeners to the sound of the electric guitar.

1943—'44
SPEEDY WEST
LAP STEEL

Pedal- and lap-steel ace Wesley Webb "Speedy" West looms large in the history of mid–20th century country music, as well as in the histories of both Bigsby and Fender. This double-neck homemade instrument is the earliest known guitar to have belonged to West. It was made in his home state of Missouri, possibly by a neighbor who lived down the street from him. This is the instrument West brought when he moved to Southern California to seek his fortune in 1946.

"It's very crude," Wheelwright says, "with ornamentation to try and make it look a little snazzier. The body is laminated mahogany, and it weighs a ton. The pickups still work. They're both hand wound."

The names *Speedy* and *West* are engraved on the two headstocks, one name per peg head. But based on his study of archival photos, Wheelwright believes that the metal *Speedy* ornament on the side was a later addition.

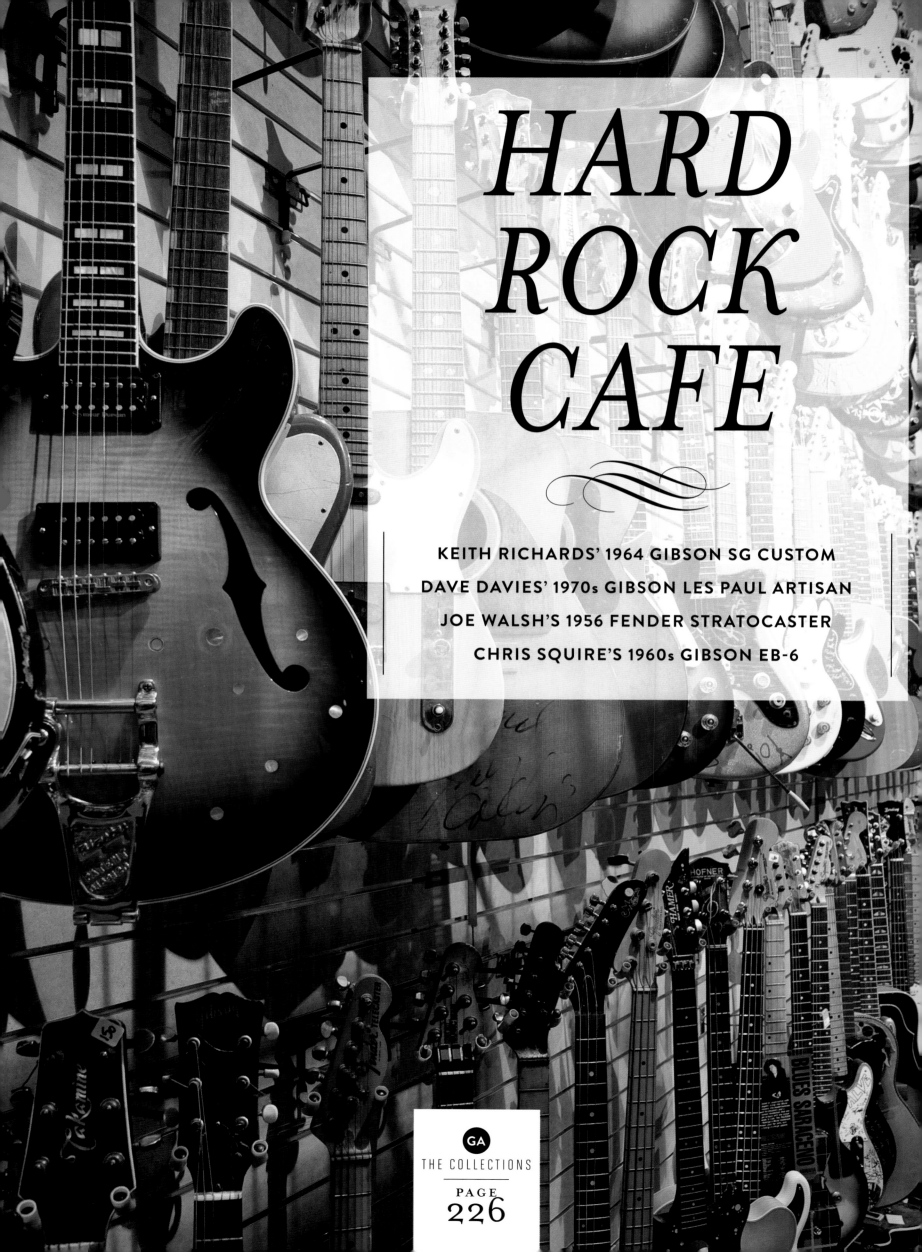

HARD ROCK CAFE

KEITH RICHARDS' 1964 GIBSON SG CUSTOM

DAVE DAVIES' 1970s GIBSON LES PAUL ARTISAN

JOE WALSH'S 1956 FENDER STRATOCASTER

CHRIS SQUIRE'S 1960s GIBSON EB-6

When American ex-pats Peter Morton and Isaac Tigrett opened the first

Hard Rock Cafe in London, England, in 1971, the now-storied establishment was meant to be a place for musicians and other industry types to congregate and make merry. The current incarnation of the restaurant as a fan mecca, replete with rock and roll memorabilia, would not begin to take shape until several years later, when one of the spot's regular customers, a certain guitarist named Eric Clapton, decided to bequeath a cheapo Fender Lead II guitar to the owners as a token of his friendship and appreciation.

The entry-level ax, which Clapton hadn't even thought to sign, was mounted on the wall as a lark, where it caught the eye of another member of Great Britain's rock royalty, Pete Townshend of the Who. Clearly feeling upstaged (and probably somewhat irked by this glaring testament to the largesse of his peer), Townshend had a black Gibson Les Paul delivered to Morton and Tigrett shortly thereafter with a note that read only, "Mine's as good as his any day." More players followed suit, and in no time at all, donating a guitar for display at the Hard Rock Cafe became a rock and roll rite of passage as meaningful as smashing one onstage.

Nearly four decades on, the Hard Rock organization has been given or acquired a staggering number of instruments and other pieces of memorabilia, all of which serve to decorate more than 157 venues in 52 countries. Jeff Nolan, the Hard Rock's online memorabilia curator, says, "One of the strange things about our collection is that it's never all been in the same place at the same time, because a large portion of it is on display all over the globe. Each location gets redecorated every seven years, so things eventually come back to our headquarters and warehouse in Orlando, Florida."

Guitars remain the heart and

The original Hard Rock Cafe, London, England, in 1973; (opposite) a wall of guitars in the Hard Rock's vault in Orlando, Florida

soul of the Hard Rock's collection, though Nolan admits that not all are equally noteworthy. He says, "The regime here in the Nineties accumulated a lot of 'signer' guitars—instruments that an artist never used and just autographed. I think we caught a bad rap for that among real vintage enthusiasts. We're still trying to reestablish the fact that we have dozens of historically significant guitars, even if they are scattered all over the planet."

To that end, the Hard Rock Cafe has launched an online web site (memorabilia.hardrock.com), where visitors can zoom in on items and examine them in minute detail. Nolan says, "When I'm in a Hard Rock Cafe and see a piece on a wall that I'm really interested in, I'll climb up on the booth to take a closer look. We wanted people to have that same sort of experience, even if the actual item is halfway around the world."

Assembling all the images and

information for the site was hard work, but it had benefits beyond what anyone had intended. "We unearthed a few important guitars that had gotten lost in the shuffle," Nolan says. A few of those instrument have rarely, if ever, been displayed before, while others, Nolan adds, "have been so far away for so long that you'd have to take a month off and cross the globe to see them." All are bona fide pieces of guitar history, wherever they may hang.

Keith Richards'
1964
GIBSON SG CUSTOM

With its white finish, gold Lyre Vibrola tailpiece, trio of gold humbucking pickups, and block-inlaid ebony fingerboard, the mid-Sixties SG Custom is one of Gibson's most dazzling and enduringly cool creations. So it's appropriate that Keith Richards, one of rock and roll's most enduringly cool guitarists, was an owner. The Rolling Stones guitarist used the instrument shown here on the 1972 tour for *Exile on Main St.* The non-original Schaller tuners suggest that the instrument might have had tuning stability issues when it was first purchased.

Dave Davies'
1970s
GIBSON LES PAUL ARTISAN

After virtually establishing the template for heavy metal with the barre chord–powered riff to the Kinks' 1964 hit "You Really Got Me," Dave Davies enjoyed three decades of success with the band. Davies' Artisan—his main guitar for all of the band's high-volume late-Seventies and early Eighties tours—is an ornate spin on Gibson's Les Paul Custom. Produced between 1976 and 1982, the Artisan has hearts-and-flowers inlays on the ebony fingerboard and the headstock, and a logo in Gibson's revived prewar-style script.

Joe Walsh's
1956
FENDER STRATOCASTER

Exhibiting the perfect amount of wear, this hardtail 1956 Stratocaster is exactly the kind of ax that owners of professionally aged reissues wish they could actually get their hands on. In addition to its bountiful vibe and patina, this particular guitar boasts a distinguished provenance, having once belonged to Eagles guitarist and onetime James Gang leader Joe Walsh. He regularly deployed it during the *Hotel California* sessions, and it can be heard on the unforgettable riff to that album's classic hit "Life in the Fast Lane."

Chris Squire's
1960s
GIBSON EB-6

Even if it hadn't been used by one of rock's greatest bass players on the 1971 prog classic *The Yes Album*, this Sixties Gibson EB-6 would merit attention simply for its rarity: Gibson made fewer than 100 examples of the instrument between its introduction in 1961 and discontinuation five years later. The EB-6 features an SG-style body, dual humbucking pickups, and oversized tuning machines. Another EB-6, previously owned by Yes guitarist Steve Howe and used by him on the 1979 *Steve Howe Album*, resides with Hard Rock as well.

The back of Stevie Ray Vaughan's
"Lenny" Fender Stratocaster,
signed by baseball Hall of Famer
Mickey Mantle (see page 242)

Beyond the Collections

A GALLERY OF LEGENDARY GUITARS

"It still had the original set of flatwound strings from
the Gibson factory on it. Plus an extra set of Black
Diamond flatwounds in the case. I still got 'em."

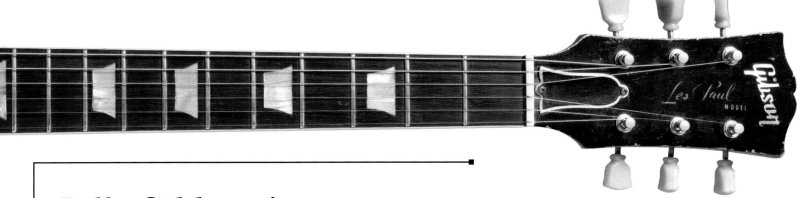

Billy Gibbons'
"PEARLY GATES" GIBSON LES PAUL STANDARD

There are few hotter guns in all guitardom than Billy Gibbons' 1959 Les Paul, known to guitar aficionados worldwide as Pearly Gates. The ZZ Top guitarist acquired the instrument in 1968, just as ZZ Top were getting underway. Pearly Gates has played a starring role on every one of the band's records, from *ZZ Top's First Album* in 1971 to the present. Threads of fortunate karma crisscross the tale of how Billy acquired Pearly. It was the seminal 1966 album *Blues Breakers with Eric Clapton* that set him on a quest to own a sunburst Les Paul like the one Clapton is seen holding in the disc's rear-sleeve photo.

"A dear friend of mine," Billy recalls, "a fellow musician, Mr. John Wilson, was playing in a band called the Magic Ring out of Houston. He told me, 'There's a rancher outside of town who played in a country band but has turned his attention toward wrangling cattle. Rumor has it that the guitar still resides under one of the beds in his ranch house.'" So Gibbons drove solo about an hour out of Houston and found the elusive rancher. "I had $250 in my pocket," Billy recalls. "And when he pulled out that '59 Burst, the deal went down."

Billy had freshly obtained the cash as the return on a favor. He'd loaned an aspiring actress a 1939 Packard automobile, which he collectively owned with some friends, so that she could drive from Houston to Hollywood for a screen test. "We didn't think the car would make it past El Paso," Billy says. "But it brought her all the way to Hollywood, and she got the part. We figured the car must have divine connections, so we named it Pearly Gates. Meanwhile, she called and said, 'Should I send the car back or sell it?' We said, 'Sell it!' She did, and my portion of the settlement arrived the very day I drove out to see the rancher."

And so the name Pearly Gates, with all its attendant magic, was transferred to the guitar, which was in mint condition when Billy obtained it. "It still had the original set of flatwound strings from the Gibson factory on it," Billy marvels. "Plus an extra set of Black Diamond flatwounds in the case. I still got 'em. Also in the case was a love note, which we also still have, from a girlfriend of the original owner. She said, 'I like what you do. Meet me later. You might like what I can do.'"

Over the years, the instrument has acquired a patina of scratches and dings, including ample belt-buckle wear on the rear of the body. Still, Billy has kept Pearly 100 percent stock. Even the frets are original. What might such an instrument be worth today? "There was a Japanese gent who offered $5 million U.S.," Billy says. "Which is an attractive offer, but then again, I've spent plenty of money putting together a collection of guitars attempting to find something to replicate Pearly, and it just hasn't happened yet. That's what led to this closet full of hardwood that I have."

Eddie Van Halen's
"FRANKENSTEIN"

Should Edward Van Halen ever decide to auction off his original Frankenstein guitar, conservative estimates are that it will set an all-time record price for a celebrity guitar, well in excess of a million dollars. Not bad for an instrument that Ed originally pieced together in 1976 from about $200 worth of spare parts.

From the Fifties through the Seventies, the vast majority of guitarists played off-the-rack instruments, and only a handful made modifications such as swapping pickups or changing electronic circuits. Eddie was the first well-known guitarist to put together his own instrument

since Les Paul scrapped together his experimental solidbody Log guitar in the late Thirties. Like Paul, Van Halen found that readily available products on the market didn't meet his needs, so he set out on his own to create a custom instrument that satisfied his exact requirements.

As Van Halen explains, the Frankenstein guitar is itself the product of his previous modification efforts. "My first real guitar was a 1968 Gibson Les Paul Standard 'Goldtop' that I bought brand new when I was 13," he says. "I later ruined it by painting it black, but that's what got me started with playing around with my guitars."

"I wanted the vibrato bar and the feel of a
Strat, but I wanted the Gibson sound. That was
a conscious move. It was not an accident."

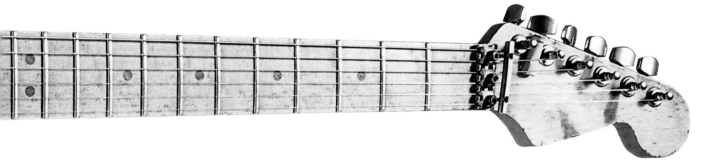

Eventually, he acquired several other guitars, including a 1961 Gibson ES-335 and 1958 and 1961 Fender Stratocaster guitars. "That 335 used to be my favorite guitar, because it had a thin neck and low action," he says. "It was real easy to play, but the guys in the band hated how it looked. It had a Vibrola tailpiece that was just a bent piece of metal that would spring back into place. I chopped that metal tail block in half, right between the D and G strings, so only the three high strings would wiggle. That way I could always go back to the three lower strings to play chords if the vibrato made the high strings go out of tune."

As whammy-bar dives became a greater part of his playing style, Van Halen discovered that the Strat's vibrato system was easier to keep in tune. Unfortunately, his bandmates considered the Strat's tone too thin. Eddie had a solution to that dilemma: he routed out the body of his 1961 Strat and installed a Gibson PAF humbucker in the bridge position. "I slapped a humbucker in there and figured out how to wire up the rest of it," he says. "That got me closer to the sound I wanted, but it still wasn't right."

All this experimentation inspired Ed to build his own guitar in 1976. At the time, Wayne Charvel and Lynn Ellsworth were making replacement guitar bodies and necks and selling them under the Boogie Bodies brand. Van Halen dropped by the factory and bought an ash Strat-style body for $50. For another $80, he acquired an unfinished, two-piece flame maple neck with a maple-cap fretboard with a 25-1/2–inch scale and 21 frets.

Because the body was pre-routed for a stock three-single-coil pickup configuration, Van Halen chiseled out a larger cavity to install a standard humbucking pickup in the bridge position. He removed a PAF humbucker from his Gibson ES-335 and mounted it to the new body—a fortuitous decision that greatly enhanced the pickup's bass response, liveliness, and sustain. Because the Strat vibrato bridge is wider than a standard Gibson Tune-o-matic bridge, the spacing of the strings and the humbucker's pole pieces didn't match. To correct this, Van Halen slanted the pickup so the low E string lined up with its corresponding bottom-coil pole piece (near-

est the bridge) and the high E string lined up with its top-coil pole piece.

One unusual "feature" of the PAF pickup in Ed's Frankenstein guitar is a broken pickup coil. "I tend to pick really hard, and when I play, the high E string always gets caught in the pickup coils," Van Halen says. "That breaks the winding on the coil. I don't know if the thing is out of phase or what, but it definitely has a unique sound. That pickup is a big part of my sound."

Van Halen installed only one pickup and a single volume control because he couldn't remember the wiring circuit for installing additional pickups and tone controls. "I never touched the tone controls anyway," he adds, "and I could never get both the neck and bridge pickups to sound right together through the amp, so I just put in the rear one." He also installed jumbo Gibson frets and a brass nut, mounted Schaller mini tuners, and salvaged a vibrato tailpiece from one of his vintage Strat guitars. Adjusting the trem, he used just three springs in a triangular configuration coming together at the three center claws in the upper retaining block. Floyd Rose had not invented the double-locking tremolo yet, so Ed developed his own detailed method for keeping the guitar in tune when using the vibrato bar. "You have to wind the strings a certain way, and the nut has to be cut differently," he says. "It's a multidimensional task."

To cover the empty pickup holes, he cut the pickguard from a piece of black vinyl. The final and most distinctive touch were the black and white stripes he applied over the body's red finish. Van Halen applied this by first spraying the body with several coats of black acrylic lacquer paint, then taping it up and spraying several coats of white lacquer paint over it. The tape was removed once the final coat was dry.

The result of these modifications was a guitar that combined Van Halen's favorite aspects of his Les Paul Standard and Jr., ES-335, and Strat. "I put a Gibson sticker on the headstock because, basically, it's a cross between my favorite features of a Gibson and a Fender. I wanted the vibrato bar and the feel of a Strat, but I wanted the Gibson sound. That was a conscious move. It was not an accident."

Eddie Van Halen's
IBANEZ DESTROYER

Eddie Van Halen may be notorious for his use and abuse of hot-rodded Strat-style guitars, but it turns out that some of his most popular riffs were recorded with this mid-Seventies Ibanez Destroyer. "I used this guitar for a lot of *Van Halen*. You can hear it on all the stuff that didn't have any whammy bar on it: 'You Really Got Me,' the rhythm track on 'Jamie's Cryin',' and 'On Fire,'" says Van Halen.

According to the guitarist, the Destroyer, which is pictured on the cover of *Women and Children First*, "was one of the few guitars made out of Korina wood that you could get without spending an arm and a leg."

Unfortunately, shortly after recording Van Halen's landmark debut, Eddie maimed the guitar in a moment of workbench zeal. "It was a great-sounding guitar—until I hacked a chunk out of it to make it look different," he says with a chuckle. "It was ruined! The sound changed from really fat and Les Paul–like to real weak and Stratty. I thought I might have damaged the pickup when I took out the wood, so I stuck in another pickup, but it sounded the same—real bad. The mistake was that I took out a piece right by the bridge, where a lot of resonance and tone come from."

Filled with remorse, Eddie went out and bought another Destroyer. "But by that time," he laments, "they'd changed the body wood."

Gary Rossington's
1959
GIBSON LES PAUL STANDARD

This 1959 Les Paul Standard has been Gary Rossington's primary guitar since the day he bought it in 1971. He's played it at nearly every Lynyrd Skynyrd concert and on nearly every album since their 1973 debut, *pronounced leh-nerd skin-nerd*. To this day, Rossington finds it nearly impossible to perform without his "baby."

"One day when we were recording *Street Survivors* in Miami," Rossington remembers, "I got lazy and left the guitar on a stand for the night. The next morning, I strapped it on, went to play, and the whole headstock just fell right off." Presumably, someone cleaning the studio the night before had knocked the guitar over, fracturing the headstock. "I started cryin' like a baby," Rossington says.

"We canceled the day's session and I took off walking. I got about a mile down the road when two friends came by and picked me up. So I went back, and the studio's maintenance man said, 'I got some glue that can fix that guitar.' And I was like, 'Glue? Man, this is a precision instrument, and it's ruined. You can have it.' I gave it to him, and when I came back the next morning, he handed me my Les Paul—fixed perfectly."

Peter Frampton's
1954
GIBSON LES PAUL CUSTOM

"It's quite surreal, isn't it?" Peter Frampton says, contemplating the return of his beloved 1954 Les Paul Custom more than 30 years after its disappearance. Frampton acquired the modified Black Beauty, one of rock's most iconic guitars, in 1970, in the midst of a three-night stint with Humble Pie at San Francisco's Fillmore West. The guitarist had been struggling to control the feedback produced by his ES-335 semi-hollowbody. After one of the shows, a fan in attendance named Mark Mariana came to the rescue, offering Frampton his modified three-pickup Les Paul to use for the final evening. "I played it for both sets," Frampton recalled of playing Mariana's guitar, "and I don't think my feet touched the ground."

Afterward, Frampton offered to buy the Les Paul; Mariana insisted on giving it to him. The guitar quickly became Frampton's Number One, making appearances on Humble Pie's classic *Performance Rockin' the Fillmore* and *Smokin'* albums, as well as on the blockbuster 1976 live record *Frampton Comes Alive!*, where it also appears in the cover photo.

Then, in November 1980, a cargo plane carrying the Les Paul and other equipment crashed upon takeoff in Caracas, Venezuela, en route to a Frampton gig in Panama. Three lives were lost in the tragedy, and all of the gear onboard was presumed lost as well. Unbeknownst to Frampton, his Les Paul had survived the crash and eventually came into the hands of a musician on the Dutch Caribbean island of Curacao, where it remained for decades. But two years ago, the unidentified player brought the instrument to Donald Balentina, a Curacao customs agent who repairs guitars in his spare time. Balentina recognized that the instrument he was looking at was something special.

"Donald said to the owner, 'You know what this is, don't you? This is Peter Frampton's guitar,' " Frampton recalls. "And the guy apparently got a little nervous. But he left the guitar overnight, and Donald took it apart and took some photos." It was around this time that Frampton was first tipped off to the Les Paul's existence. "The owner took the guitar back, and that was it," he says. "I didn't hear anything after that, and while I was happy to know that the guitar was alive, I eventually became resigned to the fact that I would never get it back."

Balentina, however, was not satisfied, and he set out to persuade the owner to sell the guitar. This past November, he finally succeeded. Unable to purchase the instrument on his own, Balentina enlisted the financial assistance of Ghatim Kabbara, a Curacao tourist board official who procured the guitar with board funds, which were subsequently reim-

Damage to the guitar included severe burns around the headstock. Removing the pickups convinced Frampton that the guitar was his. "I know those cavities!" he said.

bursed by Frampton. Together, Balentina and Kabbara flew to Nashville to present Frampton with his long-lost Number One.

"It was mind blowing to actually sit there and hold the thing again," Frampton says. The guitar showed clear signs of damage from the crash, including severe burns around the headstock and what is believed to be a point-of-impact mark near the toggle switch. But Frampton knew what he was holding. "The first thing I felt was the weight," he continues. "It's the lightest Les Paul ever. It's not chambered, but this piece of Honduran mahogany must have come from a tree at the top of a mountain, because it's so light. Then I felt the neck, which was something that Mark [Mariana] had shaved down before I ever had it. And my hands just instantly went to it, and it was like, Ooh, I've been here before!"

In addition to the guitar's light weight and shaved neck, Frampton recognized several areas of wear. "I knew the type of belt wear that I had put into the back of the body," he says. "And on the front there's a ding by the tone controls that had so annoyed me when I first made it." He laughs. "Of course, there's been considerably more severe wear and tear since then!" The guitarist had also added a Nashville-style bridge and a brass nut to the instrument, both of which were still on display.

Then there's the guitar's pickup configuration, famously modified from the 1954's factory-standard P-90 and Alnico V single-coils to a row of three humbuckers. Frampton says that merely popping out the humbuckers made it clear that this was indeed his instrument. "Back in the day, Mark [Mariana] had to have a center cavity routed out to make room for the third pickup," Frampton says. "And the two original cavities had to

be routed a bit as well to get the humbuckers in there. So when I saw the guitar—I know those cavities!"

Interestingly, it is those very pickups that have led some discerning gear heads to question the guitar's authenticity. In all Seventies-era photos of Frampton with the Les Paul, the pickup bobbins are black; on the recovered guitar they are white. But as Frampton explains, "I actually swapped out the black pickups for the ones with the white bobbins just before I left on that South American tour in 1980. That was also when I installed the white scratch plate. I put a Seymour Duncan JB in the bridge and a Duncan Custom in the middle; I don't remember what went in the neck cavity. And when I got the guitar back, those are the pickups that were still in there."

He continues. "Strangely enough, I did those mods in September of 1980, and then I decided I didn't like them, and I was going to change them back after the South American tour. But in November, the crash happened. So there was a bit of a delay!"

Currently, Frampton's Les Paul is in the hands of the Gibson Custom Shop in Nashville, where it is being restored to working condition for use on the upcoming U.S. leg of his "Frampton Comes Alive! 35" world tour. "It needs a little bit of tending to," Frampton says, "but we want to do as little work on it as possible, to maintain those battle scars." He is, however, giving the instrument a bit of an upgrade. "I'm having bumblebee capacitors and three patent-number pickups from the early Sixties installed," he says. "So in a way the guitar is going to be more authentic than it ever was. In fact, it's going to roar."

Duane Allman's
1957 GIBSON LES PAUL

Duane Allman played a gorgeous 1957 Les Paul "Goldtop" for the first 18 months of his two and half years in the Allman Brothers Band. He used the Goldtop on the band's first two albums, which featured the original versions of "Whipping Post," "In Memory of Elizabeth Reed," "Midnight Rider," "Revival," and other classics, and he performed with it on his numerous sessions with other artists, including Derek and the Dominos' 1970 masterpiece, *Layla and Other Assorted Love Songs*. Then Allman swapped the guitar for a sunburst Paul, and this piece of rock and roll history disappeared into the ether.

The story of how Duane and the Goldtop became separated is a classic tale of guitar lust. On September 16, 1970, the Allmans played a show in Daytona, Florida. Duane, fresh off recording *Layla* with

Eric Clapton and company, was, as usual, playing his 1957 Goldtop. The opening band was a local group called the Stone Balloon, whose guitarist, Rick Stine, was playing a 1959 cherry sunburst Les Paul, which caught Duane's eye. While making *Layla*, he had fallen in love with Clapton's cherry sunburst. Wanting one of his own, Duane offered to swap Les Pauls with Stine. When Stine balked, Allman upped the ante, throwing in $200 and one of his regular Marshall 50 heads.

Stine agreed, but Duane had one caveat: he wanted the Goldtop's pickups for his new Burst. The electronics were swapped, and the deal was done. Exactly one week later, on September 23, Allman played his new guitar when the Allman Brothers performed at the Fillmore East in New York City, a fact born out by video footage from the show.

"I want people to see it and hear it.
It's not my guitar; it's Duane Allman's.
I'm just babysitting."

He played his new cherry Burst throughout the rest of his career, which ended when he was killed in a motorcycle crash on October 29, 1971.

Meanwhile, Allman's original Goldtop drifted around Daytona, passing through the hands of three different owners, the last of which eventually sold it to a local guitar store. In 1977, the shop sold it to Gainesville guitarist Scot LaMar. He'd heard from his friend Billy Bowers that Duane's Les Paul was for sale in Daytona, and he rushed to the store to purchase it. He paid $475, a fair price for a vintage Les Paul in 1977.

The goldtop had some damage, including a bite mark on the headstock from a previous owner's dog. LaMar had two respected luthiers refinish the guitar, but he was dissatisfied with the results and eventually had the instrument refinished by Tom Murphy, the man behind the Gibson Historic Series and probably the most renowned "Goldtop guy" in the world. The guitar was restored to its original glory and placed on display at the Allman Brothers Band Museum at the Big House in Macon, Georgia.

The Big House Museum opened in 2010 in the communal house where various members of the band lived, played, and jammed together from 1970 to 1973. It includes thousands of artifacts from the ABB's career. The Goldtop is displayed along with artifacts directly related to it, including a shirt given to Duane by Clapton during the *Layla* sessions and two amps Duane used with the guitar: a Fender Showman and a 50-watt Marshall head, which were sometimes used together.

Other items on display include Berry Oakley's Fender Jazz "Tractor" bass and Showman amp, a T-shirt from the first-ever run of ABB merchandise, a Fender Bassman that Dickey Betts used during the band's earliest days, and one of Duane's Marshall cabs. It also includes a recreation of the famous Fillmore East stage, where the band recorded its landmark *At Fillmore East* live album in 1970. The display includes a set of vintage Ludwig drums used by Butch Trucks from 1968 to 1970, and a pair of road cases with stenciled lettering pictured on the cover of *At Fillmore East*.

"The guitar is where it belongs right now," LaMar says. "People need to appreciate it and see it."

Remarkably, LaMar's generosity with the instrument includes a firm belief that it should be played as well as viewed. "It's a real living legend and it shouldn't exist only behind glass," he says. "It's a shame to me how many of our greatest guitars have become dead artifacts."

To that end, LaMar loaned the guitar out in 2010 to Joe Davis, guitarist for the Skydog Woody Project, who used it on the group's 2011 abum, *Guitar Magic*, which also features the 1976 Gibson Thunderbird bass once owned by late ABB/Gov't Mule bassist Allen Woody. LaMar says he was just happy to see and hear the guitar being put to good use. Derek Trucks has also performed with the instrument, and LaMar hopes Warren Haynes will lay his hands on it soon as well. "I want people to see it and hear it," LaMar says. "It's not my guitar; it's Duane Allman's. I'm just babysitting."

Stevie Ray Vaughan's
"LENNY" FENDER STRATOCASTER

Purchased from a pawnshop in Austin, Texas, the beat-up 1965 Fender Stratocaster known as Lenny was more than just another a guitar to Stevie Ray Vaughan; it was an inspiration. Named in honor of his wife, Lenora, it is one of just two guitars that SRV treasured. It's also the instrument on which he wrote and always performed one of his best-loved songs: the instrumental "Lenny," written as a thank-you to his wife.

And it's the guitar that, in 2004, was sold to the Guitar Center musical instrument retail chain for $623,500, at a Christie's auction to benefit the Cross-roads Centre, Antigua, a charitable organization for addiction rehabilitation, founded by Eric Clapton.

Vaughan was not yet a star on his 26th birthday, October 3, 1980, when his wife presented him with the soon-to-be-legendary 1965 Strat. Though already a phenomenal guitarist, he was still seen as the little brother of Jimmie Vaughan, who was making a name for himself as a guitarist on the Austin circuit. The easygoing Stevie took things in stride and kept his

The backside of Lenny (shown inset) features the signature of baseball Hall of Famer Mickey Mantle, whom Vaughan met when he performed the "Star-Spangled Banner" before a Houston Astros–L.A. Dodgers game on April 10, 1985.

inlay behind the bridge. A purist would have been put off by the unprofessional custom work, but Stevie saw past that. The guitar resonated with him deeply and immediately.

Unfortunately, money was tight in those pre-stardom days, and neither Stevie nor Lenora had the $350 asking price. But with his birthday around the corner, she devised a perfect solution. "I went out and found seven people with $50," Lenora recounts, "and they all put in their money."

The guitar was presented to Stevie during a birthday celebration at the Austin nightclub Steamboat Springs, on 6th Street. He was thrilled with his new guitar and eager to play it when he and Lenora arrived home. Sometime that night, as his wife slept, Stevie wrote a new song on the guitar. In the morning, she remembers, "He was sitting on the edge of the bed with the guitar and said, 'Listen to this.'" He played her the song he had written that night: "'Lenny.' It was beautiful," she says. "How can you stop loving anything like that? I've never once in my life listened to that song without crying."

Soon after, Vaughan received a new Charvel guitar neck with a maple fingerboard as a gift from ZZ Top guitarist Billy F. Gibbons. Vaughan installed the neck on Lenny, as he now called the guitar. He also etched his name into the guitar's neck plate as a point of pride.

The song "Lenny" was included on *Texas Flood*, the 1983 debut album by Vaughan and his band, Double Trouble. SRV performed the song on his namesake instrument in the studio session; and whenever he played "Lenny" in concert, the guitarist would set aside his beloved "Number One" Stratocaster and strap on the 1965 Stratocaster his wife and friends had bought for his 26th birthday.

"It tore me up," Lenora says of her husband's poignant act. "It's so emotional for me. Overwhelming. That's a lot of love."

Among SRV's many notable live performances with the guitar was a live rendition of "The Star-Spangled Banner" at the Houston Astros' opening season game against the L.A. Dodgers, which took place at the Houston Astrodome, on Wednesday, April 10, 1985. The Vaughans were hastily flown to Houston. On the way, Stevie confessed to his wife that he didn't know how to play "The Star-Spangled Banner." In a touching example of their partnership, Lenora hummed the song as he duly noted its intricate melody. At the game, Lenora happened to be sitting next to baseball great Mickey Mantle. She introduced SRV to Mantle and, honoring the couple's request for an autograph, Mantle signed Lenora's namesake guitar, adding substantially to its collectability and market value.

Despite their love, Stevie and Lenora divorced in 1988, unable to sustain the pressures of fame and the damage from his years of drug and alcohol abuse. Vaughan, as always, continued to play Lenny, selectively and with great passion. He featured it on its namesake song, of course, and was later fond of playing it on "Riviera Paradise" from 1989's *In Step*, the album that celebrated his newfound sobriety.

Years after Stevie's death in an August 1990 helicopter crash, and at the behest of his older brother, Jimmie, Lenny became the only guitar from Stevie's estate to be made available to the public. The $623,500 Guitar Center paid for the guitar was hefty but ultimately a reflection of the effect Stevie Ray Vaughan and his music had on the people in his life and all over the world.

focus on improving his guitar playing and performance style.

It was his laidback demeanor that had attracted Lenora to him in the first place. They met at a Halloween party at the East Austin nightspot La Cucaracha, where Stevie was playing. When Lenora saw him again a couple of years later at the Rome Inn with his band, Triple Threat, she was moved both by his musical power onstage and his charmingly unassuming manner offstage.

"I kind of fell for him that day," she says. "It was tear-jerking, the guy was so good. He's so sweet when you meet him, and then he plays and he is so fierce. You can't help but feel what he feels. That was what I saw when he played."

The next time they met, at a Mexican restaurant in downtown Austin, there was no mistaking their mutual attraction. Recalls Lenora, "We looked at each other and just went, 'Uh-huh.'"

About a year after they were married, she remembers, "The guys went to a pawnshop and saw this guitar. One guy wanted it, and Stevie said, 'I want it more.'" The instrument in question was a battered 1965 maple-necked Fender Stratocaster with a rosewood fingerboard and original pickups. Although it had begun life as a three-color-sunburst model, it had been inexpertly refinished with a dark natural finish and an elaborate

Jeff Beck's
FENDER ESQUIRE

This Esquire has many claims to fame. Among them, it was used to intentionally create feedback on a pop recording, the first time that sort of thing was ever done. The perpetrator? None other than Jeff Beck, who used this instrument to create the train sounds and the sliding, shrieking guitar parts he played on the Yardbirds' "Heart Full of Soul" and "Train Kept A-Rollin'."

According to the Esquire's current owner, pickup baron Seymour Duncan, Beck acquired the guitar for $60 in 1964 from John Maus of the Sixties pop-rock band the Walker Brothers. Maus had carved a contour in the Esquire's ash body to give it the look of a Stratocaster. Beck played the guitar regularly for the next 10 years and got the most for his $60 as he established himself as one of the all-time greats of rock guitar. The Esquire was also used by Jimmy Page at certain performances during his tenure with the Yardbirds.

Beck destroyed several necks while the guitar was in his possession. The current neck was made in 1956 (the body is a 1954). In February 1974, Beck presented this guitar as a gift to Seymour Duncan, who has kept the Esquire in the exact condition in which he received it.

Ace Frehley's
GIBSON LES PAUL CUSTOM

Making his Les Paul pickups emit a cloud of smoke was part of Ace Frehley's stage act in Kiss from very early on. Unfortunately, the heat from the smoke bomb—placed in the electronics cavity—caused extensive damage to his guitars.

Eventually, Frehley had this Les Paul customized so that it would belch smoke without suffering any ill effects. "There's an asbestos-covered metal box under the rhythm pickup," he says, "a battery pack that jettisons the smoke bomb, and a halogen lamp to make the guitar look like it's on fire—though it does catch fire half the time. I never used my rhythm pickup anyway, so I converted its volume and tone knobs to trigger the smoke and light. There's also a trap door in the pickup that drops out so you can see the light."

Even so, the stunt has taken its toll on the guitar. "The neck has had to be reinforced a number of times because the metal box really heats up," he says. "It's been straightened a few times, refretted a few times, and a new fretboard was put in. But the guitar has held up, and it still sings. I record and tour with it."

Dick Dale's
"THE BEAST" FENDER STRATOCASTER

"I've only had the one guitar all my life," Dick Dale says of this battle-scarred left-handed Strat, nicknamed the Beast. The guitar has served the self-proclaimed King of Surf Guitar faithfully on every track he has ever cut, from his 1961 debut single, "Let's Go Trippin'," to 2001's *Spacial Disorientation*. The Beast is one tough animal. Most guitars would be reduced to kindling by the five decades of use and abuse the Strat has suffered at Dale's hands.

According to John English of the Fender Custom Shop, who went over this guitar with a fine-tooth comb while he was designing the Dick Dale Signature Stratocaster, the Beast was built in 1960. The original electronics have long since been modified to suit Dale's needs: an extra switch instantly engages the neck/middle pickup combination regardless of what the five-way switch is set to, and all the pots have been removed save for one volume control. Dale strings the guitar upside down with super-heavy .014–.060s.

Although the guitar used to be sunburst, Dale claims to have refinished it at least nine times in order to foil would-be copycats who, during the guitarist's early Sixties heyday, would paint their guitars to look just like his. "I used to go in and have it painted every week, just to be cute," he says. "Finally my buddy, who used to paint cars, painted it the first metal gold-flake." Dale subsequently attached two decals to the guitar: an American flag on the top horn and a Kenpo Karate emblem, which he received from his martial arts instructor.

Alvin Lee's
GIBSON
ES-335

British blues rocker and pioneer shredder Alvin Lee is best known for the extended, show-stopping version of "I'm Going Home" that he and Ten Years After played at the original Woodstock festival in 1969. He used this Gibson ES-335—which he dubbed Big Red—not only at Woodstock but also on everything from Ten Years After's 1967 debut to his 1994 solo album, *I Hear You Rocking*.

"I bought Big Red in 1963, when I was 18, for 45 pounds, case included," the late British guitarist said. "I'd always wanted an American guitar—that was the Holy Grail.

"When I bought the guitar, the pickup configuration was normal, but I immediately took the covers off to give it a little more kick and top end. I liked the Fender sound and always thought it would be great to have a half-and-half guitar, so eventually I put in a middle Strat pickup, which has a nice hollow sound. I also put on a TP-6 tailpiece with fine tuners as soon as they came out."

Lee's Woodstock triumph established his reputation—and gave Big Red one of its more prominent "tattoos."

"When I was onstage at the festival, a Woodstock sticker somehow got passed to me while I was playing, and I just slapped it on," Lee says. "The peace stickers came to me in a very similar manner in 1967 at the Fillmore West, in San Francisco, and the rest just somehow appeared. In 1973, I broke the neck off, and when they replaced it they also relacquered the guitar, so the stickers became permanent fixtures, which is fine."

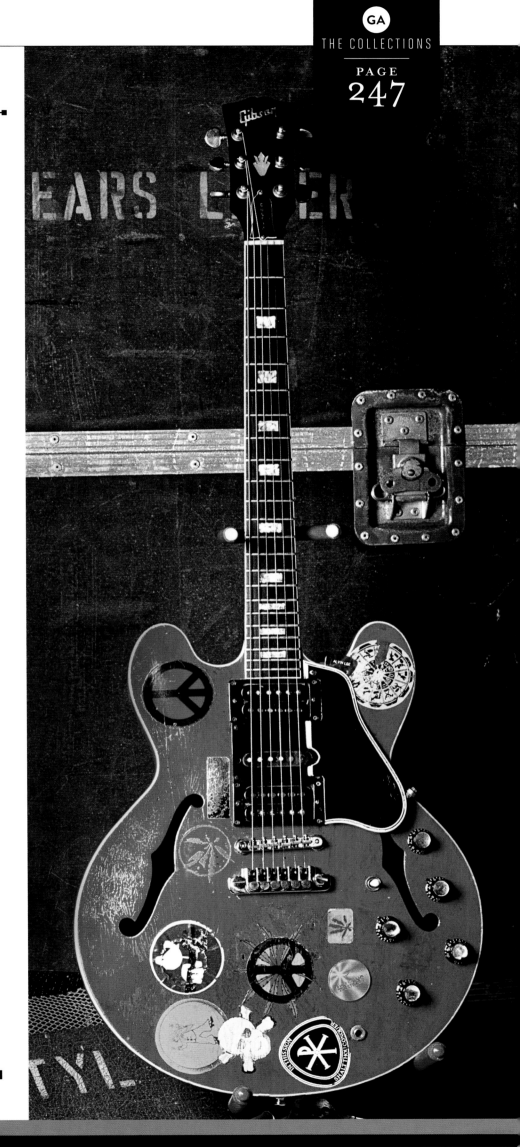

Yngwie Malmsteen's
"DUCK" FENDER STRATOCASTER

This 1972 Stratocaster, nicknamed the Duck, is easily the most celebrated of Yngwie Malmsteen's guitars. He bought the guitar in the late Seventies, in his native Sweden, from a drummer auditioning for his band. "It's not my favorite Strat," the neoclassical shredder says, "but for some reason it's one of my best-sounding ones. It's been my main guitar since '78."

Malmsteen used the Duck almost entirely when he played with Steeler and Alcatrazz in 1983. The guitar has also appeared on the covers of numerous Malmsteen albums and is the guitar he used to play all the solos on his Grammy-nominated *Yngwie J. Malmsteen's Rising Force*, from 1984. He played the instrument on all of his tours until he retired it from roadwork in 1995.

Like most of Malmsteen's Strats, the Duck is fitted with DiMarzio HS-3 pickups in the bridge and neck positions, with the original pickup still in the middle, and the standard Fender bridge. The maple fingerboard was scalloped by Yngwie himself in 1980.

The guitar has seen more than its share of use and abuse over the years. In 1987, while Malmsteen was performing in Anchorage, Alaska, "an overenthusiastic fan threw a half-empty one-liter bottle of Jack Daniels onstage and hit the 17th fret so hard, it popped right out of the wood," he recalls. He subsequently had the guitar refretted with Dunlop 6000 frets.

However, much of the guitar's damage has been inflicted on it by Yngwie himself. "The headstock has broken off at least six times, and I used to put my cigarettes out on it all the time," he says. "I'm not very kind to my instruments. Sometimes I'll throw my guitar high into the air, but a spotlight may get in my eyes when I try to catch it. So rather than let the guitar break my hand, I let it crash onto the floor."

Steve Howe's
GIBSON
ES-175D

Steve Howe turned the heads of many of his fellow guitarists in the early Sixties by using what was widely regarded as a jazz guitar in a blues-and-rock format. He bought this classic Gibson ES-175D in 1964 when he was performing in a London-based blues group called the Syndicats. Howe continued to use the 175 in his next three bands: Tomorrow, a short-lived outfit called Bodast and, finally, in Yes.

"Although my first electric guitars were a Guyatone and a Burns Jazz, the ES-175D was my first Gibson guitar and represented the start of a long love affair with Gibsons," Howe says. The guitarist used this particular ES model throughout his celebrated career with Yes, one of the most adventurous progressive rock groups of the Seventies. He used this classic instrument on such standout Yes tracks as "Heart of the Sunrise" and for the final solo in "Siberian Khatru."

Howe fondly remembers when Bodast played a support gig with Chuck Berry at the Royal Albert Hall, in London, in 1969. "I got a chance to ask Chuck what he thought of my 175," he recalls. "He picked it up, strummed it a bit, and said, 'This is great, a lovely guitar.' So I put the guitar back in the case and felt really good. Chuck Berry played my guitar!"

Tony Iommi's
GIBSON SG

"I bought my Gibson SG in a music store in Birmingham, England, back in 1967," says Black Sabbath's Tony Iommi. "I was told it was a '64, but I've never verified that. Originally it was my backup guitar—my primary guitar was a Fender Stratocaster. While I was recording the first track on our first album, the Strat's pickups blew. I couldn't find anyone who knew how to repair it, and we didn't have replacement parts in those days, so I just trashed it and started using the SG. It sounded good, so I never looked back. It was my primary guitar on *Black Sabbath*, *Paranoid*, and *Master of Reality*."

Iommi did little to alter the SG during the years he recorded those albums. Later, however, he customized the Gibson with the aid of guitar maker John Birch. "I replaced the bridge pickup with a handwound John Birch humbucker," he explains. "Birch was a craftsman who designed and modified guitars for me when companies refused to meet my demands. Besides winding custom pickups for my instruments, he also built my first 24-fret guitar when others said it was impossible."

The cherry-colored, fire-breathing ax has spent its golden years in the mustachioed metal master's closet, though Iommi does pull it out from time to time. "I still use it in the studio occasionally," he says. "My biggest problem with the instrument is that it has a very weak neck. It actually goes out of tune as much as a half step if you apply too much pressure on it."

Brian May's
RED SPECIAL

Brian May designed and built his Red Special guitar when he was a teenager, and it has been his main guitar ever since. He played it on every Queen album and tour as well as on numerous side projects and his solo albums.

May and his dad began work on the Red Special in 1962 and took two years to complete it. "I was 17 when it was finished," he says. "I knew I wanted a guitar that would sing and have warmth as well as a nice articulating edge. We tried to design a solidbody guitar that had all the advantages of a hollowbody—the ability to feedback in just the right way."

The Red Special is a masterpiece of inventive domestic craftsmanship. A motorcycle kickstand provided the spring in the vibrato tailpiece, while the oak body came from a 500-year-old fireplace mantel. The massive neck—May has big hands—contributes to the Red Special's trademark warm sustain. So does the unique switching system that May designed for the instrument's three single-coil Burns pickups. Each has its own on/off switch and phase switch, making it possible to effect a broad spectrum of tones.

"It's very well-suited to that violin sort of tone that I use to build up 'guitar orchestras,'" May says. "That sound was a dream from childhood—I could hear it in my head." Under the circumstances, it's not surprising that May hasn't traded the Red Special for any other instrument. "I figure it's gonna last just about as along as I do, with any luck."

In 1969, Page paid Joe Walsh just $500 for the
classic 1959 Standard pictured here. Today, similar
instruments regularly fetch sums of six figures.

Jimmy Page's
1959 GIBSON
LES PAUL STANDARD

The Les Paul Standard's original designers and manufacturers—including Les Paul himself—would no doubt have been shocked by the veneration heaped on the guitar. Upon its introduction in the early Fifties, it was received with only moderate enthusiasm. But with the coming of the second generation of rock guitarists, the reputation of sunburst Les Pauls built between 1958 and 1960 skyrocketed. Besides Page, other greats who have played these guitars include Peter Green, Dickey Betts, Ace Frehley, and Keith Richards.

With the guitar's increase in desirability came a concomitant rise in price on the vintage guitar market. In 1967, one could cruise into the old Dan Armstrong shop in New York's Greenwich Village and stroll out with a tiger-striped 1959 Les Paul for $750. Around April 1969, Page paid Joe Walsh just $500 for the classic 1959 Standard pictured here. Today, similar instruments regularly fetch sums of six figures.

John Lennon's
1964
RICKENBACKER
325

The Beatles' August 1965 performance at Shea Stadium ranks among the most famous rock concerts in history. Though most of the audience couldn't hear the music above the screams and general hysteria that persisted throughout the show, they could at least see the Beatles—and John Lennon's black Rickenbacker 325.

Lennon bought his first Rickenbacker 325 in 1960, when the Beatles performed in Hamburg, Germany. After using that guitar extensively onstage and in the studio, he was given this guitar, his second 325, by Rickenbacker when the Beatles first came to America, in February 1964. This model featured a new vibrato bar and a five-knob control layout. Lennon first played his new 325 in public during the Beatles' second appearance on *The Ed Sullivan Show*, broadcast live from the Deauville Hotel in Miami, Florida. The guitar was first used in the studio on "Can't Buy Me Love," recorded a few weeks later.

Les Paul's
LOG

In 1941, Les Paul built the now-legendary Log, a working solidbody instrument that he continued to tinker with and improve for years to come. At the instrument's core is a four-by-four pine "log," which is surrounded by Epiphone sides. The guitar's back is a piece of plywood fastened to the body with several flathead screws. The instrument's pickups were fashioned from an old electric clock. At 20 pounds, the Log feels more like a wrought-iron girder than a guitar. In fact, it was too heavy for Paul to lug around on tour, but when he did take it to a show, he would wow his audience by removing the sides.

For all the Log's notoriety, its true historical significance is extremely difficult to determine. Contrary to popular belief, the Log was not the first solidbody guitar. In fact, at the time it was built, the Vivi-Tone company made a full line of solidbody electrics, and almost a decade earlier Rickenbacker had produced a solid Bakelite lap-steel guitar that Paul himself was photographed playing on various occasions. In addition, the Log did not influence later solidbody designs, not even those of the Gibson guitars that sported Les' moniker.

The real explanation for all the buzz about the Log is Les Paul himself. He is, after all, the man whose name adorns one of the most popular guitars ever made. He was also a highly successful recording artist who did much to popularize the electric guitar. More to the point, the guitar he played from 1941 to 1949 on his string of hits, as well as on several Bing Crosby records and on the road with the Andrews Sisters, was the none other than the Log, making it one of the most significant guitars of the past century.

GUITAR
A F I C I O N A D O

EDITORIAL

EDITORIAL DIRECTOR
Brad Tolinski

EDITOR-IN-CHIEF
Tom Beaujour

MANAGING EDITOR
Christopher Scapelliti

ART

DESIGN DIRECTOR
Danielle Avraham

ASSOCIATE ART DIRECTOR
Patrick Crowley

PHOTOGRAPHY DIRECTOR
Jimmy Hubbard

DIGITAL IMAGING SPECIALIST
Evan Trusewicz

BUSINESS

VICE PRESIDENT, PUBLISHING DIRECTOR
Bill Amstutz

GROUP PUBLISHER
Bob Ziltz

CONSUMER MARKETING

CONSUMER MARKETING DIRECTOR
Crystal Hudson

AUDIENCE DEVELOPMENT COORDINATOR
Kara Tzinivis

FULFILLMENT COORDINATOR
Ulises Cabrera

MARKETING COORDINATOR
Dominique Rennell

NEWBAY MEDIA CORPORATE

PRESIDENT & CEO **Steve Palm**

CHIEF FINANCIAL OFFICER **Paul Mastronardi**

CONTROLLER **Jack Liedke**

VICE PRESIDENT OF PRODUCTION & MANUFACTURING **Bill Amstutz**

VICE PRESIDENT OF DIGITAL MEDIA **Joe Ferrick**

VICE PRESIDENT OF AUDIENCE DEVELOPMENT **Denise Robbins**

VICE PRESIDENT OF CONTENT & MARKETING **Anthony Savona**

VICE PRESIDENT OF INFORMATION TECHNOLOGY **Anthony Verbanac**

VICE PRESIDENT OF HUMAN RESOURCES **Ray Vollmer**

TIME HOME ENTERTAINMENT

PUBLISHER
Jim Childs

VICE PRESIDENT, BRAND & DIGITAL STRATEGY
Steven Sandonato

EXECUTIVE DIRECTOR, MARKETING SERVICES
Carol Pittard

EXECUTIVE DIRECTOR, RETAIL & SPECIAL SALES
Tom Mifsud

EXECUTIVE PUBLISHING DIRECTOR
Joy Butts

EDITORIAL DIRECTOR
Stephen Koepp

DIRECTOR, BOOKAZINE DEVELOPMENT & MARKETING
Laura Adam

FINANCE DIRECTOR
Glenn Buonocore

ASSOCIATE PUBLISHING DIRECTOR
Megan Pearlman

ASSOCIATE GENERAL COUNSEL
Helen Wan

ASSISTANT DIRECTOR, SPECIAL SALES
Ilene Schreider

SENIOR BOOK PRODUCTION MANAGER
Susan Chodakiewicz

DESIGN & PREPRESS MANAGER
Anne-Michelle Gallero

BRAND MANAGER
Katie McHugh Malm

ASSOCIATE PREPRESS MANAGER
Alex Voznesenskiy

SPECIAL THANKS

Katherine Barnet, Jeremy Biloon, Rose Cirrincione, Jacqueline Fitzgerald, Christine Font, Jenna Goldberg, Hillary Hirsch, David Kahn, Mona Li, Amy Mangus, Kimberly Marshall, Nina Mistry, Dave Rozzelle, Ricardo Santiago, Adriana Tierno, Vanessa Wu

SUBSCRIBER CUSTOMER SERVICE: **Guitar Aficionado Customer Care, P.O. Box 469030, Escondido, CA 92046-9030**
WEB SITE: **www.guitaraficionado.com/customerservice** PHONE: **1.800.825.2234** E-MAIL: **guitaraficionado@publink.com**

BACK ISSUES
Please visit our store: www.guitarworld.com/store or email at guitarworld@nps1.com

EDITORIAL AND ADVERTISING OFFICES
28 East 28th Street, 9th Floor, New York, NY 10016 PHONE: **212.768.2966** FAX: **212.944.9279** WEB SITE: **www.guitaraficionado.com**

NEWBAY MEDIA, LLC
28 East 28th Street, 12th Floor, New York, NY 10016 WEB SITE: **www.nbmedia.com**

CONTRIBUTING PHOTOGRAPHERS

James Bland (Gary Rossington's Gibson Les Paul Standard) • **David Bowman** (Brian Setzer) • **Adam Chandler** (Hard Rock Cafe) • **Max Crace** (Eric Johnson) • **Jeremy Danger** (Joe Bonamassa) • **E.J. Devokatis** (Duane Allman's Gold Top) • **Stan Evans** (Lynn Wheelwright) • **Mike Graham** (Rick Nielsen) • **Michael Grecco** (David Crosby) • **Ross Halfin** (James Hetfield, Eddie Van Halen's Frankenstein) • **Jimmy Hubbard** (Randy Bachman, Elliot Easton) • **Karjean Levine** (Dick Dale's "The Beast" Fender Stratocaster) • **Dale May** (Steve Earle) • **Ari Michelson** (Robbie Robertson) • **Nigel Osbourne/Redferns/Getty Images** (Steve Howe's Gibson ES-175D, Jimmy Page's Gibson Les Paul Standard, John Lennon's Rickenbacker 325) • **John Peden** (Billy Gibbons' Pearly Gates, Jeff Beck's Fender Esquire, Les Paul's Log) • **Jonathan Pushnik** (Rich Robinson) • **Matthew Rainwaters** (Jimmie Vaughan) • **Rayon Richards** (Jim Irsay) • **Robert Knight Archive/Getty Images/Redferns** (Stevie Ray Vaughan's "Lenny" Fender Stratocaster) • **Kevin Scanlon** (Lindsey Buckingham, Jakob Dylan, Mick Mars) • **Michael Sexton** (Eddie Van Halen's Ibanez Destroyer) • **Travis Shinn** (Neil Giraldo, Peter Frampton's 1954 Les Paul Custom) • **Jonathan Sprague** (Carlos Santana) • **Lorinda Sullivan** (Ace Frehley's Les Paul, Tony Iommi's Gibson SG, Brian May's Red Special) • **Kim Tonelli** (Alvin Lee's Gibson ES-335) • **Roderick Trestrail II** (Brad Whitford) • **Neil Zlozower** (Yngwie Malmsteen's "Duck" Fender Stratocaster)